STORAGE

A HOUSE & GARDEN BOOK
STORAGE

Writer: Melinda Davis

Editor: Barbara Plumb

Designer: Albert T. Hamowy

Pantheon Books · New York

Published in the United States by Pantheon Books, a division of Random House, Inc.,
New York, and simultaneously in Canada by Random House of Canada Limited,
Toronto.

Library of Congress Cataloguing in Publication Data

Davis, Melinda.
    Storage.

    "A House & Garden Book."
    1. Storage in the home.   I. House & Garden.
II. Title.
TX309.D38   1978   684.1′6   77-88766
ISBN 0-394-42681-9

Manufactured in the United States of America   First Edition

Contents

Acknowledgments _____ 6

Introduction _____ 7

1
Storage Systems _____ 8

2
Storage Shelves _____ 28

3
Architectural Storage _____ 46

4
Special Storage _____ 68

5
Decorative Storage _____ 88

6
Storage Devices _____ 100

7
Kitchen Storage _____ 118

8
Bedroom Storage _____ 134

9
Bathroom Storage _____ 152

Acknowledgments

I would like to express my thanks to Louis Oliver Gropp, Editor-in-Chief of *House & Garden Guides,* to Paul Bonner and Priscilla Massie of the Condé Nast Book Division, to William Rayner of The Condé Nast Publications Inc., and of course to Barbara Plumb of Pantheon Books. Special thanks are due to Albert Hamowy, Art Director of *House & Garden Guides,* who designed the book and contributed much creative energy.

To the Condé Nast editors who discovered and developed the original stories that inspired this book, special recognition is due: Mary Jane Pool, Editor-in-Chief of *House & Garden,* and her staff in New York and across the country; the editors of *House & Garden Guides;* of British *House & Garden* (London); of *Maison & Jardin* (Paris); and of *Casa Vogue* (Milan). Not to be forgotten are the owners, designers, and architects whose taste and creativity inspired the original stories, and the photographers who recorded their subjects with equal aplomb.

Thanks also to designer David Stiles, who provided much of the technical information in the book, to Carol Knobloch of *House & Garden Guides,* to Jeanne Morton, Connie Mellon, and Phyllis Benjamin of Pantheon Books, and to Carol Kageyama of the Condé Nast Foreign Department.

Melinda Davis
House & Garden Guides

Introduction

Limited space and a need to impose some sort of order on our possessions are two realities we all face in designing our personal environments. No one ever seems to have enough space; it is a commodity that may well become our greatest luxury, not only in traditionally crowded urban areas, but everywhere across the country as available space diminishes and housing costs soar. Planning for the most efficient use of this limited space is, of course, what makes all the difference. Superb organization can make even the tiniest square footage extravagantly serviceable, and in large places as well as small, order greatly enhances livability. Well-designed storage schemes are a first step.

It is little wonder that many of the first furniture designs were developed as storage devices. In the Middle Ages, people were not burdened with a great many possessions, partly because there were no easy means for producing things in great quantity, partly because the powerful Church was hostile to unnecessary possessions and there were sumptuary laws that limited conspicuous private consumption. Nevertheless, storage was an important concern. What possessions people did have that were not in constant use were put away on the ground floor of the house in a storeroom that shared the space with stables and perhaps an armory. One all-important piece of furniture at the time was the chest. People carried entire households about with them as they followed the court or the hunt. Nearly everything they owned went into portable packing chests, and at each destination these chests became essential furniture — both for continued storage and for seating and tables. Only when life became less itinerant and different rooms in the house developed specific functions did more elaborate furniture come into being. At some point before the Renaissance, the chest evolved into the cupboard: shelves were added on top, along with front-opening doors. As time went on, furniture became increasingly specialized for storage: card tables with drawers, sewing tables with hidden bins, linen cupboards adapted from the tall units used to protect firearms and powder from the damp. By the eighteenth century, a great number of specialized storage pieces had developed: Bible boxes, armoires, campaign chests, secretaries, sideboards, hutches, desks, breakfronts, chests of drawers.

Most of the needs that inspired these storage designs are still with us today, but we have added a rather extraordinary array of new ones. More products and possessions have made their way into our lives, requiring new methods for storage. Consider a family with a shared interest in up-to-the-minute entertainment equipment— amplifiers, speakers, tapes, and records. One member may be involved in sports, another in photography, another in crafts, another in cooking. Each has a sizable collection of books on his or her subject, and each shares in a wide assortment of community possessions, from bed linens to a wine collection. The storage challenges are obvious, and architects and designers are meeting these challenges with a great burst of energy and creativity.

This book brings together some of the most innovative storage solutions that are to be found in America and Europe, as well as some of the best traditional solutions, all gathered by an international staff of Condé Nast editors. Because it is in the nature of today's storage designs to be specialized, each chapter deals with a specific, specialized approach: storage systems, where several parts work together as an extremely efficient whole; storage shelves, the basic building block of nearly all systems, in all their glorious flexibility; and architectural storage, where the design of storage solutions is considered an integral part of the total design of a space. One chapter is completely devoted to designs for special, hard-to-store items: collections, wines, firewood, stereo equipment. Another deals with storage that is at least as important for its decorative value as for its efficiency — especially noteworthy because all the designs in this book were chosen for their visual appeal. The chapter on storage devices—or storage stratagems—shows how to use one large piece of furniture, like a cupboard, or one great idea, like hanging baskets from the ceiling, to fit the storage design to the item stored. The final three chapters deal with specific solutions for the kitchen, the bedroom, and the bathroom. Throughout the book are ideas for carrying out the designs yourself, or for caring for them once they are complete. Care was taken to make the book equally appropriate for the person who is planning a new space and looking for the ultimate storage system to begin with and for the person who is looking for new ideas to supplement storage he or she already has. All are presented in the belief that handsome, well-designed storage is one great way to bring order and good looks to your personal environment.

1
Storage Systems

Stacking cubes for books —
Stair-step bookcases —
Room-dividing shelves —
Panels and boxes — Full wall
systems — Modular units —
Built-in antique cabinets —
Floor-to-ceiling built-ins —
A systematic apartment —
Roll-around space dividers —
Make-it-yourself tower cabinets

Storage systems are great triumphs of synergistic efficiency. Each unit of a well-planned system works quite well on its own, but when it is put together with other devices — or more of the same — the total effect is greater than the sum of the parts. Storage systems fall roughly into two categories: those that are built-in and those that are portable. Some are both — designed to be built-in in one space, then carried away and built-in in another. The range of possibilities is enormous. Whether planned by a professional or put together by yourself, systems are the ultimate in custom-designed storage solutions.

Modular units to buy or build are standardized, proportionate pieces. They stand side by side, fit in wall recesses, hang from the wall, or stack, and can be increased, decreased, or totally rearranged as needs change. They can be moved when you move.

Some systems serve more needs than just storage, with desks and serving counters and even beds incorporated in the design. Some also work as room dividers, serving more than one space at a time. Others are total rooms unto themselves. Pushed to its greatest potential, a system can not only provide the storage requirements within a room but also contain and conceal the room itself, as is the case with the kitchen behind doors in the chapter on decorative storage.

To be a system, parts need not physically connect, but only be part of a total scheme. A full wall of cabinets in one part of a room supplements open shelves in another to create the most efficient total system for the space. And though the streamlining of storage made possible by systems is usually associated with streamlined contemporary design, the idea is appropriate to traditional rooms as well. An early system of built-in cabinets and drawers, long noted for its practicality and unfussy good looks, is an American Shaker design — circa 1790.

a system of cubes

One basic storage device, the cube, is multiplied to create the most traditional storage system of all, storage for books. Contemporary design turns the cubes on a diagonal, making the system a spectacular showpiece for the room. An added bonus of the diamond pattern: oversize or undersize books that seem out of place on ordinary shelves are no problem here, where smooth horizontal lines are no longer a mainstay of the design. Designer: Giovanni Patrini.

DAVID MASSEY

stair-step bookcases for a bedroom

Above: In a bedroom of total built-ins, even the bed becomes a part of the
storage system. Ascending, stepped-up modular bookcases continue
the full length of one wall; complementary descending mirrored paneling
covers the wall space not claimed by the shelves. The carpeted platform
that extends from the bookcases serves as a bedstead (carpeted
fold-down lids conceal extra storage space) and incorporates a mattress
for sleeping. Designers: Kahn & Mallis Associates.

eye-level bookcases dividing a room

Left: A system of bookcases that lines a wall on one side of an apartment
room and serves as a partial room divider on the other manages to provide
enormous storage potential without overpowering the room. Because
of the height of the units — just below eye level — the room divider does
not greatly inhibit the flow of space and light. Architect: Gae Aulenti.

Idea: Use 90° angle braces to attach
each vertical unit of stepped-up bookcases to the next. One arm of the
angle is screwed to the top of the first
case; the other arm is attached to the
side of the second case.

panels and boxes for a home office

The key element of this library-study system is a full-height wall panel with evenly spaced horizontal grooves into which other components fit. Simple shelves and rectangular boxes — in varied sizes and with or without doors — create the storage complex arranged on the panel. More cases continue across the wall. The desk itself, with its fitted, detachable drawers, is part of the total system, as are the file boxes on casters that are used as side tables for more-than-one-function efficiency. In designing such a system, one approach is first to list all the items that must be stored, then to list the units into which they best fit. The final step is to arrange the chosen units for accessibility and visual appeal. Storage-system components by Behr International.

Idea: The most professional way to hang rectangular box bookcases on the wall is to use beveled hanging strips. These strips are attached both to the wall and to the back of the bookcase. The strip on the case hooks into that on the wall for an extremely close fit and solid support the length of the wall.

a double row of shelving

Right: An open-corridor storage system was created by lining one entire wall with wooden shelves mounted on metal standards and brackets, then installing a parallel stretch of shelves a few feet out from the wall. The standards for these latter shelves are heavier, but the shelves, also mounted on metal brackets, are the same. A partial wall of glass helps define the corridor. Architect: Michael Leonard.

JOHN WINGROVE

eight components, one study

Left: Black-stained ash is used consistently for all the components of a corner-study grouping. In this arrangement of rearrangeable units, three bookcases are stacked, two cabinets are placed side by side, a desk consisting of file-cabinet bases and a writing top is placed at right angles to the basic storage components. In a different space, the units could all be placed against the wall — even all in the middle of the floor. Storage-system components: "5000 Series" by Fristho of Holland.

Idea: Heavy items such as hardcover books and records require special consideration when stored on long shelves. Two-inch-thick nominal lumber provides greater stability than plywood for shelves. There is less of a problem with sagging, and such thick shelves require support only every 3 feet. (Less substantial shelves should be supported every 2 feet if they are to hold heavy books or records.)

a desk plus shelves for a study wall

Left: More standards and shelves, this time in combination with a long bench desk, establish a home office center. Such a system could take advantage of an existing recess in a wall, or the entire wall could be constructed from scratch as a room divider, using the depth of the wall not claimed by shelves for cabinets. The desk, if hung on brackets, should be supported at least every 2 feet. Designer: Marc Baurand.

JOHN WINGROVE

stacking library units

Above: In a fresh white room designed to be cool and uncluttered, a half-wall of shelves keeps objects organized and under control. The system comprises nine separate components: eight library units of white-painted ash and the plinth they are stacked upon. For a quick change, the units could be placed side by side along the full wall to form a buffet (a second plinth would be necessary), the paintings hung side by side above them.

modular storage for a modular room

Right: The storage systems in this single room for living and dining are modular, and so is nearly everything else. (The sofa can be pulled apart, the chairs pushed together.) Five identical bookshelves — easily built or inexpensive to buy — offer almost limitless flexibility. Cylindrical plastic stacking units can be stacked to the ceiling or unstacked one by one to be used as side tables. Interior designer: Gary Crain.

Idea: For a more permanent arrangement, fasten modular bookcases through the side with screws. They will still be easy to disassemble, but much less wobbly in appearance.

ERNST BEADLE

built-in cabinets from historic America

Built-in storage is not a strictly modern concept. New England Shakers in the eighteenth century, with their passion for order and functionalism, became known for their expertly crafted, specialized storage furniture—much of it built in, like the unit above in the parlor of a Shaker house in Massachusetts. In reproducing such a system for a traditional room today, it is important to remember that the Shakers usually designed theirs to be asymmetrical—but perfectly balanced—with a minimum of hardware and no decorative cornices or moldings.

and from modern Europe

Floor-to-ceiling built-in cabinets line the walls in an unquestionably contemporary European library. Two devices make this system unique. So that objects stored may remain visible and therefore easy to retrieve, the doors have grillework rather than solid panels. So that objects, if need be, may be concealed, window-shade-type panels inside the grillework can be raised or lowered at will. Flexibility is enormous; the look of the room can be changed in minutes. Redecorating is a matter of changing the panels. Designer: Jacques Grange.

Idea: If you can spare 1 foot each in the length and width of the room, increase storage space by lining two walls with built-in cabinets. . . . **Idea:** Build doors like those above of 1×4 clear pine and 1-inch-square wire mesh, mortised into the door.

a total system for an open-plan apartment

When an apartment with seven tiny rooms was gutted and remodeled
as one large, interflowing space, few walls remained to support
conventional storage devices. A new, total system was required. The
remaining wall space was taken over for cabinets and closets that
unobtrusively use every inch to best advantage. A freestanding
system of cabinets, bookcases, and drawers was added as a low room
divider that not only helps define spaces but also serves as an
important decorative element. Designers: Studio Zziggurat.

and how it works

Opposite above: To the left, a wall of black plastic laminate that conceals the kitchen contains a row of low cabinets. To the right, a modular system of cabinets, bookcases, and drawers helps divide the room without closing it off. Opposite below: A view through the kitchen toward the room divider. One black panel folds down to open the kitchen to the seating area and to serve as a bar. Below left: Even the bathroom wall contains recessed storage. Below right: A view of the kitchen wall with the bar panel folded down. Bottom: In a long entrance hall, the walls on either side are lined with closets.

Idea: To reproduce the look of burnished metal for closet doors, use plastic laminate with a metal finish to cover ordinary hollow-core doors.... **Idea:** To conceal built-in storage in a bathroom, apply tile to match the walls to the door of the unit. Use a touch latch rather than hardware for the door.

monumental units for space engineering

In a living room that is a complex of angles—many corners, high and low ceilings, an end wall concealing stairs that is itself stair-stepped—several freestanding storage units of varying heights can be rolled about on casters to vary the space even further. The units themselves are unusually uncompromising, with shelves and compartments specially constructed to hold best each item stored. In this arrangement (two views above), they are placed library-like behind one sofa, some presenting an open side, some a closed side. Two units of different dimensions stand sculpture-like beneath a dropped ceiling (right). Even the coffee table has a swing-up door concealing extra storage space. Architecture, interior design, storage units, and coffee table all by Cini Boeri.

Idea: For rolling storage cabinets, build units 2 inches shorter than the desired finished height to allow for carpet casters.... **Idea:** The units can be completely sheathed in plastic laminate or painted with semigloss enamel. For the smoothest painted finish, build units of ½-inch birch plywood, spackle and prime before painting.

compartmentalized, wall-hung tower cabinets

Many storage experts consider full-height cabinets the most practical and efficient single storage units of all. At work counters, they do not crowd headroom as overhead cabinets might, and they provide easy access without revealing things one might not want revealed. This versatile system of seven separate wall-hung towers (they could line an entire room) has the look of fine modern design while being extraordinarily utilitarian. One key to its success is the flexibility of the dimensions of the compartments. The depths of the units vary, so it is not necessary to dig through paraphernalia in front to reach what is stored in back. The shelves are adjustable; even the drawers can be installed at any point. Because the units are totally mobile, they can be easily lifted for cleaning, switched from room to room, increased or decreased as needs change, and taken along in moving. Designer: Martin Lipsitt. (These were built to order by Amron, New York.)

a versatile system that you can build yourself

The wall towers on these pages, designed to hang together on a wall bar, were all made of unfinished white birch plywood. They grade from 7 inches wide and 8¾ inches deep to 15¾ inches wide and 18½ inches deep. While this system is arranged for dining-room storage, the units, with their fully adjustable shelves and great design flexibility, could be adapted for storage for any purpose. The doors swing open in two directions, and should be notched for easy opening.

Idea: To simplify home building of the wall towers, draw a plan to scale (1 inch equals 1 foot) and take it with you to the lumberyard. Have the pieces cut to your specifications from ¾-inch cabinet-grade white birch plywood. This saves sawing at home and makes transporting of the wood easier.... **Idea:** Use three pivot hinges on each door. Treat the wood with at least three coats of polyurethane for a natural, durable finish.

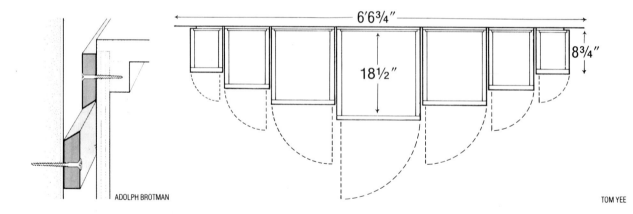

6'6¾"

18½"

8¾"

ADOLPH BROTMAN

TOM YEE

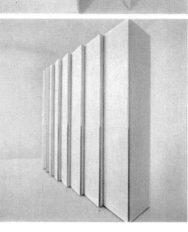

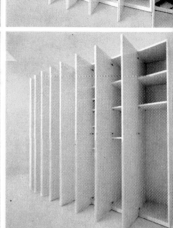

flexible floor-tower cabinets

The ultimate in cabinet adaptability is offered by these flexing towers on glides that can stand straight against a wall, swing in a circle, divide a room, even create a curving room within a room. One complete system as shown here provides storage space equivalent to a conventional 8-by-2½-foot closet, 2 feet deep. But compartments of varying dimensions put more space to work and increase accessibility. Designer: Martin Lipsitt.

to build the system yourself:

These cabinets, like those pictured on the two preceding pages, are made of white birch plywood (shown here lacquered white). Each individual tower is angled. Their dimensions vary from the smallest, which is 8 inches deep on its most shallow side, 11½ inches on the opposite side, and 6½ inches wide, to the largest, which is 19½ inches deep on its deepest side and 14 inches wide. The total system measures 6 feet 8¾ inches long and 6 feet 5 inches high. Each unit rests on four glides, so a screwdriver adjustment is all that is required to level them on an uneven floor. Towers are slip-pinned together at top and bottom so that they unfold like a piano accordion.

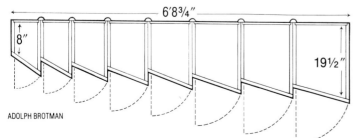

6'8¾"

8"

19½"

ADOLPH BROTMAN

Idea: For a lustrous finish for tower cabinets, build them of plywood and paint them with sealer before sanding. After sanding, spackle the entire surface, then sand again and prime. Finish with enamel spray paint. (Three quick, thin coats are better than one thick one—they dry faster and are less likely to run or streak as they dry.)

TOM YEE

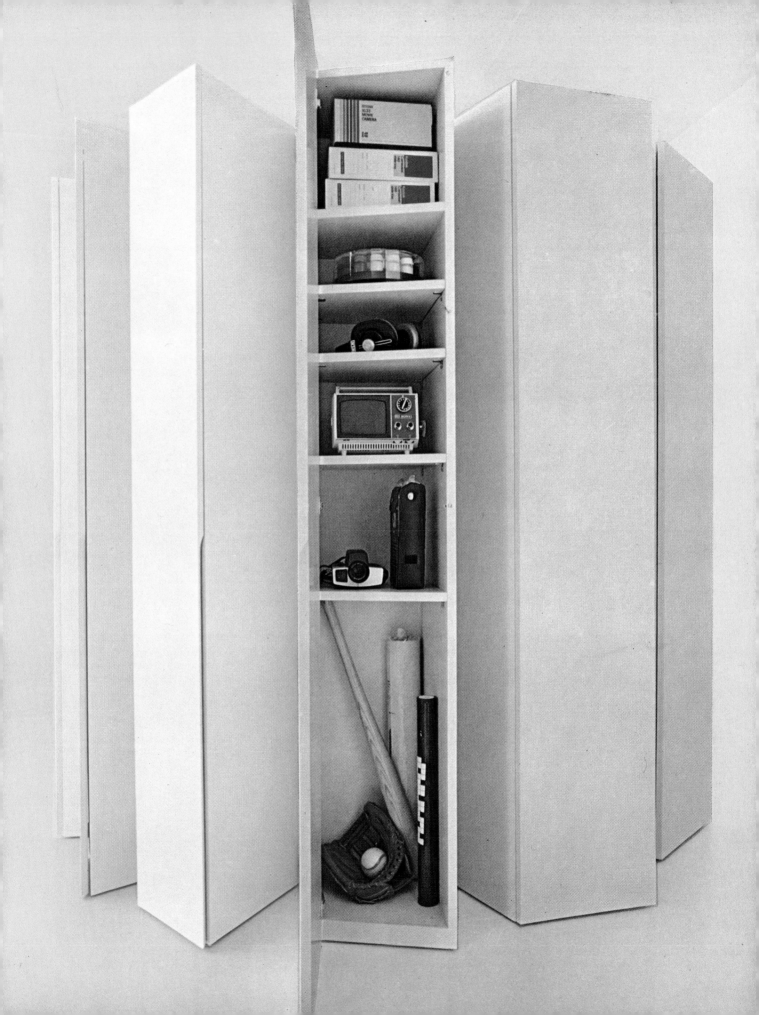

2 Storage Shelves

Shelves for books — For art —
For objects — For collections —
For kitchen equipment —
For liquor — For entertainment
systems — Shelves framing a
doorway — Lining a wall —
Flanking a fireplace — Standing
free — Filling a room — Shelves
made of wood — Of metal —
Of glass — Of acrylic plastic —
Of industrial components —
Of old utility drawers — Shelves
with mirror, special lighting

Shelving is, of course, the basic building block of all storage systems, the most fundamental answer to the problem of where to put things. At the most primitive level, shelves are a simple device. Rather than spreading our possessions about on the floor, we cut out smaller spans of supplementary floor space and stack them up until we have a place for everything. At the most sophisticated level, shelves have evolved as a functional art form and can be the key design element in a room.

Much of the excitement in shelf design right now comes from the wide variety of materials being used. Shelves of hardwood, softwood, plywood, or fiberboard are still a good choice — often the best. But some designers are also sculpturing shelves out of styrofoam or plaster, molding them in heavy plastic, constructing them of industrial components chosen for both their practicality and their honest good looks. For shelves to display fragile *objets d'art,* more delicate-looking glass or clear acrylic plastic is appropriate and can be stunning in its own right, especially when combined with rich metals, mirrors, and special lighting.

Shelves can almost always be a do-it-yourself project. If they are mounted with standards and brackets on plaster or wallboard, the standards should always be attached directly to the studs. To find these vertical inner-wall supports, measure from a corner of the room in 16-inch increments until you reach a suitable spot for the first standard. Using a masonry bit, drill a hole until you hit the stud. If you don't, carefully probe inside the wall with a straightened wire hanger or other flexible instrument.

Keep drilling trial holes until you hit a stud dead center — holes can be filled with a little plaster later. Screw the standards directly to the studs, using long self-tapping screws and washers. (Screw length should equal the combined thicknesses of wall and standard plus one inch for best support.)

Versatility is the greatest asset of shelves. Where they go, what they hold, what they are made of, how they look—it is all up to you. Here are some ideas.

shelves framing a doorway

Metal bookshelves framing a doorway create a dramatic, deep entrance to a bedroom. In the room they directly serve, the shelves are a bar, a stereo center, side tables for magazines and fruit, as well as a place to keep books. An especially effective design decision for this thoroughly contemporary setting: the walls behind the shelves, as in the bedroom, are painted black. Designer: William Cavendish.

EDDIE RYLE HODGES

shelves in an open-plan apartment

Left: A double row of shelves on either side of a room in an open-plan apartment changes function as the room definitions subtly change. In the kitchen, the shelves supplement cabinets and hold liquor, glassware, and the most attractive cooking utensils. Near the desk, they hold books and reference material. In the living area, they display art and hold a stereo speaker. Interior designer: Nina Gabo.

in a dining room– cum– family center

Right above: When the dining table is a family gathering place and the center for many activities, ample storage nearby can be crucial. Here, deep shelves from wall to wall hold everything from trinkets to photographic equipment. With the addition of a lamp and a stool, one well-placed shelf is a desk. Interior designer: Jill Dufwa.

in a kitchen– cum– dining room

Right below: Shelves are used in combination with a buffet cabinet unit in the dining area of a kitchen dining room. Placement of the shelves takes advantage of the dropped ceiling over one wide doorway. The wall that rises above the doorway at one point serves as a bookend for extra-tall volumes. Architects: Richard Rogers, & N W Foster.

Idea: To mount the standards for shelves on masonry walls, drill oversized holes with a masonry bit and insert a lead anchor in each hole. Screw through the center of the standard into the anchor; the anchor expands in the masonry wall and holds tight.

RICHARD EINZIG

JAMES MORTIMER

shelves in recesses flanking a modern fireplace

Recesses on either side of a clean-lined contemporary fireplace provide space for built-in bookshelves of equally sleek design. Spacing of the shelves is uniform and uncomplicated—for storage of records on the left, the usual-size space is simply halved horizontally. Space along the top of the shelf unit could be used for outsized books or left empty for a clean architectural look. Exterior latex paint (more heat-resistant) is best for the fireplace. The shelves, to match, could be painted with the same. Interior designer: Sophie de Kinkelin.

Idea: To help keep white-painted shelves clean, wash them thoroughly with mild soap and water or spray cleaner, allow to dry, then buff with a very light coating of paste wax to prevent dirt from sticking to the surface. Dusting will prolong the time between cleaning and waxing.

along one wall in a sitting room

Below: Shelves are combined with cubes, speaker cabinets, fold-down-front cabinets, and even drawers in an apartment sitting room. The arrangement is asymmetrical—one key to its marvelously casual look. Placing furniture in front of the shelves underlines the fact that the system is indeed a wall and must not overpower the room. (Only the most infrequently used articles, of course, should be stored behind the furniture.)

PHILIPPE LEROY

JACQUES BACHMANN

drawers as shelves to house a collection

Printer's drawers, clean-painted and attached to the wall behind a bar, become a display case for a vast collection of matchboxes gleaned from years of travel. Drawer compartments form shelves that appear made to measure for the small items and frame each box as a popular-culture work of art. (Note the large box that was divided to fit into the shelves.) Designer: Ristomatti Ratia.

Idea: Look for dentist's, printer's, or apothecary's drawers to salvage as wall units.... **Idea:** Drawers can be hinged on one side to form decorative doors for other storage units (attach stored objects with sticky tape).... **Idea:** Attach drawers to the wall with molly or toggle bolts or heavy screws, depending on the type of wall construction.

JOHN WINGROVE

industrial-look stereo shelves

Left: Factory parts—man-made and proud of it—are becoming increasingly popular in interior design. Here, a floor-to-ceiling shelf unit with the look of the factory holds equipment from another area of technological know-how: electronic entertainment components. The metals used here are not, of course, the usual heavy-duty steel, but such an authentic factory product could easily be used for the same purpose. Designers: David Resnick Associates.

bedroom shelves from a warehouse

Right: Real industrial shelving is used to form a near-total wall of storage for books, magazines, and stereo equipment. The shelves, originally designed for warehouses, are capable of holding great weight without warping. Pre-drilled holes simplify assembly and make shelf arrangement extremely flexible. Interior designer: Ristomatti Ratia. Architect: Ilkka Salo.

a custom bar unit

Below: A rather spectacular bar unit in the spirit of industrial shelving is glorified with the use of fine steel and copper and elegant curves. The unit is freestanding; access is from the rear of the shelves. Architect: Gianfranco Fini.

Idea: Buy industrial components from factory supply outlets, industrial equipment catalogues, restaurant and hospital supply companies. . . . **Idea:** Spray-paint the metal units with rustproof paint. . . . **Idea:** Coasters to protect carpeting are important when using metal standards, especially if the items to be stored are very heavy.

CHRISTINA GHERGO

one big room for kitchen storage

Storage is more than an integral part of the design of this room; it is the very reason for its design. Black plastic-laminate shelves are supported by adjustable metal brackets and standards. Each section of the room is reserved for specific items. From left: bar equipment and accessories, serving dishes, a tier of plates, table-setting accessories, food staples, cookware and appliances. On the third wall, in the mixing bowl section, is an artificially lighted greenhouse; above the communication center is a cookbook library. Baskets hold fruit, linens, small utensils, and silverware wrapped in protective cloths.

Idea: To plan a kitchen storage room, first list each item you have to store, then categorize according to the best method for storage: stacking, hanging, arranging on a shelf or in a basket. Estimate the amount of space required for each. Draw a plan to scale, mapping out a place for each array of shelves, each hook, each basket, each partition.

an étagère of glass and chrome

Left: Objects displayed on this glass étagère might appear to be suspended in midair were it not for the narrow strip of chrome across the front of each shelf. Small items that could be lost in a grid of heavy wooden or metal shelves are appropriately displayed in this more open arrangement. The unit itself seems to claim less space in the room. Designer: Harve Oeslander.

stacked cubes of glass for a collection

Right: A collection of *objets d'art* can be viewed from all sides when displayed in a freestanding stack of glass cubes — an appealing study in delicacy itself. The vitrine-cubes, open at the front, can be easily rearranged as the collection changes. The unit is fragile: only the bottom shelf, supported directly by the floor, can carry the weight of light books. Glass cubes by Roche-Bobois.

Idea: To make your own glass cubes, have plate glass cut to measure and assemble with ready-made connectors from hardware stores, or … **Idea:** Make your own connectors with thick strips of acrylic plastic. Use a table or radial-arm saw to make dado cuts on three sides of the plastic, wide enough to fit the thickness of the glass.

glass shelves for a balcony art gallery

Above: In an elegant living room where background colors are pale and mirrors on two sides of the room play with light and image, the art objects on glass shelves appear almost to float. Shiny metal posts that support an interior balcony along the fully mirrored wall also support the individual thick glass shelves. Another shelf is suspended between the wall and the upper railing of the balcony. Designers: John Michael Design Consultancy.

a mirrored niche with lighting from above

Left: Placing mirror on an adjacent wall doubles the impact of a figurine collection displayed in a niche fitted with glass shelves. Mirror behind the shelves reveals the back of each figurine and reflects light from the built-in overhead fixture. Because the shelves are transparent, it is possible to light all the objects from above with a single fluorescent tube that is partially concealed behind the upper framing of the case. Designer: Marc Bohan.

Idea: For glass shelves to support art objects (not recommended for books or records), use ⅜-inch plate glass. Shelves should be supported every 2 feet.... **Idea:** It is now possible to buy fluorescent tubes for display lighting that require no special wiring—just attach and plug them in.

a triangular étagère in a corner

Right: Triangular glass shelves are supported by round floor-to-ceiling posts in a corner étagère for both art and books. Because the supports are not attached to the walls, the unit is easy to place in the corner—claiming an unexpected bounty of space—and does not interfere with the drawing of draperies. Designer: architect Alberto Pinto.

steel, glass, and brass shelving

Below: An uplight hidden behind a tortoise shell displayed as art makes the floor-to-ceiling stainless steel standards of a shelf unit gleam, its glass shelves mounted on brass bands sparkle. On the adjacent wall: a matching frame of stainless steel. Both are reflected in the glossy deep aubergine of the ceiling. Interior designer: Olivier Brunard.

JACQUES PRIMOIS

J. BACHMANN

Idea: For shelves, a 3-foot span of glass should be ⅜ inch thick; the same length of acrylic plastic should be ¾ inch thick.... **Idea:** Cut acrylic plastic with a table saw, finish edges by sanding.... **Idea:** Never dust acrylic plastic with a dry cloth. Clean it with a weak solution of dishwashing liquid, rinse, and wipe with a cotton cloth. Remove grease with naphtha. Never use window cleaner, strong solvents, or abrasives, which can cause damage.

plexiglass shelves for twin niches

Above: On either side of a smoky plexiglass door, transparent plexiglass shelves teamed with chests turn deep niches into display space. Indirect lighting from lamps atop the chests makes the thick edges of the shelves a glowing white (glass edges would be green)— a dramatic effect against white porcelain. For continuity, the same smoky material used for the door covers the walls on either side of the niches. Interior designer: Gilbert Edard.

complete transparency for a wall unit

Right: A wall unit constructed totally of glass allows the beauty of a high-relief parget wall to show through. A single cylindrical spot on the floor provides light from below, both illuminating the objects on the shelves and casting shadows that enhance the texture of the wall.

3
Architectural Storage

High-reaching shelves—
Storage at ceiling level—
Platforms for storage—Full
walls of shelves—A room within
a room—Shelves dividing a
space—Shelves emphasizing
form and line—Storage as
a graphic element—Storage for
color in architecture—Shelves
recessed in a wall, in a niche

What makes architectural storage different from any other large-scale storage system is its relationship to the space it serves. In the first, the line, form, and proportion of the system and their effect on the rest of the space are as carefully envisioned as those of the room itself. Often they are wholly integrated: storage is part of the very structure. Storage systems can be added to a finished room with great effectiveness and style. But to add an architectural system is to redesign the space.

As with architecture in general, architectural storage expresses our view of the role of shelter now. More and more people are choosing open-plan living spaces. In such a setting, storage structures can be a way of differentiating activity areas, of subtly controlling the flow of space and light, or of accentuating the height or depth or volume of the space. An architectural system can be a room within a room.

Where the architect's aesthetics demand that free objects be kept to a minimum, storage becomes part of a total, pared-down design where even furniture is spare and built in. As color becomes more important in architecture, we are beginning to see storage solutions that are as remarkable for the graphic color they provide as for the utility they afford. Materials as well are chosen from an architectural point of view. When the architect's purpose is to relate the structure to the site or to express an affinity for geographical or cultural heritage, this applies as much to storage as to the rest of the interior, and we see shelves of local materials, such as adobe or stone.

In modern architecture, storage design can be a way of introducing historical allusion. In a remodeling, it can reinterpret an old, existing motif—such as an arch in an updated Victorian house. As easily as it can be part of the walls, storage can be part of doorways and windows. At times, the very reason for a room is storage: structure and storage device are one. In all cases, the role of architectural storage is the same: to be an effective working part in a well-designed machine for living.

two-story bookshelves

That these shelves hold books is almost secondary, for they are above all an architectural element in a high-reaching room of carefully engineered space and light. One sees not the shelves but the space around the shelves, as their vertical stroke of color emphasizes dramatic height. Architect: Paul Rudolph.

Idea: To create a long, unbroken horizontal line of shelves near the ceiling, use heavy wire to hang the shelves from screw eyes firmly fastened into the ceiling frame. If the shelves are to hold books, space the wires no more than 16 inches apart.

ceiling shelves sweeping around a room

Left: In a spectacular brownstone apartment remodeled with platforms, mirror, glass, and light, a sweep of overhead shelves provides storage for books. Central to the design of the apartment is the minimizing of freestanding objects. Not only do these shelves become an unobtrusive part of a totally built-in environment, they also make use of an often overlooked space: the ceiling. Architect: Paul Rudolph.

ceiling shelves traversing a room

Above: Rectangular-box shelves as thick as the dividing walls of the apartment—and in the same color—not only hold books but seem to support the ceiling as they line the top of one wall. Perpendicular to this line is a double shelf in graphic red, the design suggesting the forms of structural beams. Interior designer: Stephanie Mallis Kahn. Architect: Douglas Kahn.

TOM YEE

49

creating a room within a room

Instead of partitioning off a small bedroom section in a one-room apartment, the designer created a freestanding room within a room. With the doors closed (top), the 7-foot cube looks rather like a large-scale sculpture. Having it placed at an angle makes it easy for the eye to travel around and above it, preserving the large proportions of the room. Behind the doors (right), the cube is an enclosing, private space for sleeping. Beneath the bed is storage space for linens and stereo equipment. Above: For everything from dishes to clothing, the designer built a row of 16-inch-deep closets with uniform doors to maintain the uncluttered flow of the wall. Architect: Timothy Wood.

Idea: Build the sides and doors of this sleeping cube of 2 × 4 framing sandwiched between two layers of hardboard. Support the bed with a cross-framing of 2 × 4's every 3 feet. . . . **Idea:** For mobility, use four heavy-duty casters beneath the four corners of the cube.

WILLIAM GRIGSBY

RICHARD GLOUCESTER

a bedroom—study wall for a student

Above: To effectively divide sleeping and work areas, yet allow the two spaces to remain joined parts of the same room, a deep bookshelf wall is open on both sides. One large opening allows a window to be shared by both spaces. The top shelves hold bulky stereo speakers and items of least frequent use. The entire unit is of simple wood framing—easy to build, easy to remove when the function of the room changes.

a study wall for a musician

Left: A collection of more than ten thousand records is stored on the wall of one musician's study. The shelves extend from wall to wall, from floor to ceiling, and are painted black to remain as much a part of the background as possible. A desk niche in the wall supplements the larger desk that is placed to look like an extension of the shelves. Another shelf is reserved for stereo equipment — all close at hand.

Idea: To divide a room with open shelves, special-order long pieces of plywood to reach from floor to ceiling. Support the shelves on simple brackets nailed to the plywood.... **Idea:** To save space when storing large record collections, buy album boxes that hold six record sleeves each, label them on the side, and file like books.

bookshelf walls enclosing a work space

In the middle of a long living-dining room complex is an unexpected
room-within-a-room with walls of white-lacquered wooden bookshelves.
The idea: to create a secluded working environment within the bookshelf
walls and at the same time provide display space for a large collection
of art on the outer side of the shelves. The walls are subtly angled
and stop just short of the ceiling to avoid a drastic interruption
of the larger space. Architect: Gae Aulenti.

traditional shelves enhancing an archway

When a Victorian house was remodeled, it gained a new arched opening over a library door, inspired by the original arched shapes in the house, like the Palladian window in the next room. Bookshelves around and above the door subtly continue this arch motif and set the stage for yet more storage: lighted niches to display art, cabinets built in below the niches, two banquettes with storage space below. Architect: Warren Cox.

Idea: For concealed lighting to illuminate sculpture displayed on shelves (see opposite), use strip fluorescent lighting on the ceiling of the shelf, hidden behind a 1 × 3 fascia board painted to match.

55

HENRY CLARKE

a white-painted wood activity-room wall

Left: An expanse of shelves serves as a dividing wall to set apart a living room designed for many purposes: reading, entertaining, even swimming. The wall comes just short of reaching the ceiling, so adjoining rooms still subtly interflow. Interior designer: François Arnal.

a light wood hallway wall

Below: In the long hallway of a centuries-old Danish house, shelves of natural-finish light wood line an exterior wall. The shelves vary in size to suit the items stored; the entire system is interrupted occasionally to frame existing windows. Interior designer: Ib Rasmussen.

a walnut library wall

Opposite: Bookshelves reach the full height of a fourteen-foot ceiling in a library designed as a family living center. Although the room is enormous, the mood is warm, owing partly to the books themselves, partly to the material the shelves are made of. Dark-stained walnut was used for the shelves, the walls, and even the floor. Architect: I. W. Colburn.

Idea: For exceptionally high shelves like those shown opposite, install a library ladder that slides the full length of the shelves, using barn-door-type hardware. Such hardware comes in two parts: a track that is attached to the wall of the barn, and ball bearings that are attached to the door itself. For this purpose, fasten the track to the shelves, the ball bearings to the top of the library ladder.

TOM YEE

JENS BULL

shelves as an important graphic element

Right: Much of the drama of this contemporary apartment comes from the repeated theme of straight lines interrupted by curves — the strong, straight lines of the room itself and the curving lines of the furniture, for example. The storage scheme establishes this theme: a glass and aluminum shelf system with a vividly graphic look, dominated by a sweeping curve that leads the eye toward the window and the view. On a balcony overlooking this living and dining room (above), the theme is taken up in reverse for a shelf system serving a design table. Architect: Bruno Sacchi.

Idea: To make a curved panel for bookshelves like these, use a saw to make a series of kerf cuts across the board—the greater the curve desired, the closer together the cuts. Create a smooth, finished surface by covering the curved board with thin, flexible plastic laminate.

strong horizontal lines in a soaring space

Below: In a living space beneath a spectacular sloping ceiling, a wall of built-in bookshelves is as much an architectural element as a tall curving staircase, a skylight, many windows, and a balcony. Tucked beneath the floor of the balcony above, the bookshelves help define one area of the larger space. Designers: William and Serpil Rosenfeld.

Idea: The space beneath the bottom shelf in a full wall of bookshelves is often wasted. It can be put to efficient use as a storage space for a long line of wooden bins (as shown opposite), boxes on casters, large baskets, or special cubes that hold record albums.

a horizontal line turning a corner

Above: Multiple planes and bold angles—emphasized by recessed lighting—help give this library corner of a living room its drama. Sleekly contemporary black bookshelves turn the corner but stop just short of the ceiling, their clean horizontal line an effective contrast to the many levels and angles of the ceiling. Architects: Ernesto Griffini and Dario Montagni.

bookshelves in a wall of adobe

Left: This two-story living room of adobe and pine is nearly 30 feet square. Space definitions derive partly from the arrangement of the furniture, but more basically from the design of the walls. Here, pine bookshelves for a work area are recessed directly into the adobe wall. Designer: Kipp Stewart.

shelves for food in a wall of stone

Right: A great deal of the excitement of this strikingly modern house comes from its clean geometric lines and natural materials. Open storage in the kitchen—dining room works with this scheme. Natural wood shelves are a part of the stone wall—there is nothing to clutter or complicate the strong lines of the room. The decorative element is the food itself. Architect: Stanley Tigerman.

Idea: For either of these built-in units, construct the bookcase before building the masonry wall. Set the bookcase in place, cover it with a protective sheet of plastic, then build the wall around it, using mortar to help hold it securely in place.

MORLEY BAER

ROBERT LAUTMAN

rich color against white

The bare bones of this bedroom were left frankly exposed, showing off their functional handsomeness. Within the white, almost industrial-looking shell of the room, the red-lined bookshelves provide a bold stroke of color. The bright tone is concentrated in a single horizontal stretch rather than over the entire wall, so it does not overwhelm the room or dilute its own strength. Architect: Barton Myers.

GOLA STUCCHI

many colors against black and white

Above: For a child's room, huge building-block structures serve as both storage and furniture. Color underlines the strong geometric lines of the design and helps make the room an extremely personal environment. The child's favorite colors — painted on the back walls of the giant shelves as well as on the ceiling — are vivid against walls of pure black or pure white. Architects: Franco Giorgetta and Giuseppe Pagano.

white against rich color

Below: To make a tiny apartment seem larger, one unifying color and texture was used throughout. Red carpet covers everything but the walls and tabletop; carpeted platforms and cubes serve as most of the furniture. The overhead shelf is an important part of the scheme. Placed high, so that it does not interfere with the flow of space, and painted white, it is a strong, graphic stroke of contrasting color that adds punch to the rest of the room. Designers: Kahn & Mallis Associates.

JAMES MATTHEWS

Idea: If you prefer not to paint, use vinyl, felt, or other fabric to line open shelves with color. Some vinyl wall coverings can be peeled off and used again. Fabric can be attached with an ordinary office stapler.

CRISTINA GHERGO

TOM YEE

twin niches with fabric panels

In a bedroom anteroom that is little more than a niche itself, panels of fabric and treillage make the most of shallow niches in the curving walls. Shelves of painted board placed in the niches are at varying heights in order to accommodate the Art Nouveau objects and lamps as well as books. If such niches do not already exist, it is possible to mimic the effect by building out the wall with similar fabric panels and putting up shelves. Architect: Mongiardino.

Idea: To construct real niches where none existed before, locate the studs in the wall (see the chapter on shelves, page 28) and carefully chop out a rectangular hole between them. Use 1×6 clear pine to frame the niches and build shelves (in a house with standard framing, the shelves will be 14 inches long). Finish with spackle and paint.

66

mirrored niches
rounding corners

Right: When an old living room became a new dining room, rounding the corners was part of the transformation. First wallboard was curved around the corner; then niches were tucked into the space. Mirrors help display *objets d'art* but also play subtle tricks with the dimensions of the room. Architect: Warren Cox.

a horizontal niche
with a stroke of color

Below: Two windows with unimpressive views were removed to make a long, narrow niche that now holds plants and art objects in a city apartment dining room. The walls of the niche are painted yellow; the stripe of color angling around the corner is a bold graphic element in the design of the room. For parties, the ledge becomes a buffet. Interior designer: Merrill Scott. Architect: Yann Weymouth.

ROBERT LAUTMAN

4
Special Storage

A tower for firewood—Shelves and a column for entertainment equipment—A system for personal memorabilia—
A place for skis, hats, artist's supplies, crafts materials—
Display and storage for art and photography—
A systematic room for abundant miscellany—Shelves, racks, and cellars for wine.

Just as there is a great abundance of new possessions, there is an explosion of new storage design: exceptional, even experimental designs that were never thought of before—and never could have been—simply because they were never before needed. At the same time, possessions that have been with us a long time are being treated differently as we change the way we live and change our personal living spaces. Firewood is hardly a new item to have in a house, but a living space that is a sculptured, multilevel modern cave is certainly new, and so we have an innovative molded tower to store its wood.

Home entertainment equipment is almost a standard item, and even elaborate systems are becoming increasingly common. Challenged by this proliferation of miniature mission control centers, designers have come up with great storage solutions: keep it undercover until it is used; display it in all its electronic glory; claim a space with storage structures to give the equipment a room of its own. Many leisure-time interests are seeing similar upswells and similarly original storage solutions.

Not long ago, few Americans had even heard of Pouilly-Fuissé. Today, in great numbers, they are stocking it away, so even old ideas for storing wine are new again. Sports equipment needs a place to go, as does all the paraphernalia associated with crafts. The trick, as always, is to keep it accessible—though protected, attractive, and out of the way.

Art is a very special possession that requires special techniques for storage. Some designs place it front and center in avant-garde displays; others are more traditional; all are correct. The key is how well they suit the way you live. And what of those devoted collectors of personal memorabilia, great batteries of equipment, pretty things chosen simply to please? Professional designers and collectors have found ways to both systematize and enjoy such treasures—the crucial concern for every specialty in this chapter.

a dramatic tower of wood

Firewood storage becomes sculpture in a room that is a true adventure in form and space. The staircase and columns are welded steel, braced, then covered with plaster, carved, and gilded. The funnel-shaped chimney is steel and cement. As wood for the fire is extracted and replenished, the tower—as functional art—is constantly redesigned, resculpted.
Interior designer: Jay Steffy.

JAY STEFFY

shelves to reveal everything

Below: A grid of black shelves that extends the length of the living room uses compartmentalization to keep a vast collection of books and records organized. Individual selections can be removed without risking the balance of an entire shelf of books. Specially sized compartments provide permanent places for television and stereo. Decorative panels take the place of shelves along the hard-to-reach lower border. Designer: Peter Preller.

ACHIM DEILING OSTRINSKY

Idea: When designing a built-in storage wall for entertainment systems, take accurate measurements of each piece of equipment. Remember to include space for reaching the rear controls of the television and for raising and lowering the dust covers of turntables. Carefully plan the location of electrical outlets.

doors to hide everything

Right: A designer who prefers to de-emphasize objects in small rooms placed an entire entertainment complex — stereo system, television, records, and tapes — as well as a library on a full wall of shelves that can be instantly hidden behind sleek black touch-lock doors. With all the doors closed, the room is simply furnished with a sofa and a coffee table. The doors can be selectively opened to reveal one unit at a time — or all. By graphics designer Gilbert Lesser.

TOM YEE

a column for music and movies

Above: A freestanding column in a hallway solves one of the most challenging storage problems: how to keep entertainment systems at hand without creating an electronic eyesore. Three sides of the column open (below) to reveal projectors, film reels, tape deck, turntable, amplifier, records, and tapes (speakers are in the living room); one side is vented. Interior designer: Norman Diekman. Architect: Lee Harris Pomeroy.

a sound-system wall

One solution for entertainment equipment is to design a separate structure devoted to nothing else (above). A second solution (right) is to integrate it totally into the room. Here, stereo apparatus becomes almost a part of the wall. Aluminum bookshelves are recessed into the bright red-lacquered walls. One unit continues from the floor to the ceiling. Interior designer: Michel Boyer.

Idea: When designing recessed shelving for stereo systems, allow sufficient space for ventilation and for wires that are attached in the rear. **. . Idea:** Use a telephone-wire staple gun to fasten speaker wires to baseboards when speakers are set up at a distance of more than a few feet from the amplifier.

DAVID MASSEY

collection shelves and cupboards

Opposite and right: Very personal memorabilia are the special items to be stored in this combined living-dining-working room. A high overhead shelf displays a collection of figurines; cupboards hold commemorative china, books, and souvenirs; a desk cabinet provides space for film reels and notebooks and a spot for children's art on its open door. Designer: Priscilla Baschieri.

collections in a study corner

Below right: In the same apartment, a study corner outside the bedroom is decorated with a hanging collection of primitive weapons. Other bits of collections — a tiny statue, a shell—are interspersed with books in a generous shelving system. The idea here and throughout the apartment: collections need not be set apart in elaborate display cases, but can be placed here and there to create a very personal setting.

Idea: To create a ceiling shelf for a collection display, cover the entire ceiling with plywood paneling (here with a vertical groove) and extend the paneling to form a ledge. For lightweight objects, a simple wooden post is sufficient for support.

CHRISTINA GHERGO

MARIS-SEMEL

a ski center of boxes and rocks

Left: At entry level in a winter vacation house, the combination of a rocky but solid boulder floor and open-box shelving makes the perfect center for putting on, taking off, and storing ski boots and other equipment. Open boxes keep everything visible and mildew-free; the spaces between them offer support for skis. Rock ledges serve as benches; dirty drip runs off so that winter mess is little problem. Architects: William Rienecke and David Sellers.

Idea: To hang painted plywood storage boxes from a concrete wall, use masonry anchors that expand in the wall and panhead screws. The greater the weight, the larger the anchor necessary. For boxes of this size (above), four #10 1¼-inch screws would be adequate.

a hallway ski center

Right: A hallway is transformed into a ski room with the simple addition of a floor-to-ceiling rack. Vertical wood standards anchored to the wall have sturdy wooden spokes projecting at regular intervals. Skis are laid across the spokes. The distance between the support spokes depends, of course, on the length of the shortest skis to be hung. Interior designer: Jane Bell. Architect: Brett Donham.

ERNST BEADLE

a hanging hat collection

Above: Storing and displaying a collection need not always mean investing in glass-fronted cases. This collection of straw hats is well cared for on the wall — protected from crushing and misplacing. On top of that, the collection becomes an important, lighthearted element in the dining room of a vacation house.

a system for an artist's studio

Right: The original beams of a remodeled barn help form the framework for a storage wall in an artist's studio. Rolls of canvas are filed away in a system made of Sonotubes, heavy cardboard molds used for concrete pilings and structural columns. Stretched canvases slide between rough-sawn vertical posts. The inner surfaces of the posts are covered with carpeting to protect the canvases. Owner/designer: Kenneth Noland.

baskets for a workroom

Above: A tiny niche of a room with a window became an efficient work space with the addition of a shelf-box-and-basket system and a desk. The room is the center of a great deal of activity — writing, bill paying, correspondence, crafts. All of the necessary paraphernalia is stored in baskets or wallpaper-covered boxes close at hand on the shelves, easing a potential clutter problem that could overwhelm the small room and adding a light touch that makes the room a delight to work in. Interior designer: Alexandra J. Stoddard.

and for a crafts room

Right: For a family of craftspeople, an entire large room is set aside for sewing, painting, drawing, and batiking fabric, the idea being that serious craftswork needs its own space with materials close at hand. Once again, the mainstay of the design is a combination of shelves and baskets. Each basket holds one work in progress or materials related to one activity. Room clean-up is simple: clear the worktable into a basket, file the basket on the shelves. The bottom shelf of the system creates a neat niche for a row of file cabinets.

Idea: For thick, substantial-looking shelves that do not burden a wall with great weight, use flush hollow-core doors cut in half lengthwise, then painted and hung on standards and brackets. Depending on what you plan to store, it may be necessary to reinforce the hollow shelves with small blocks of wood just inside the newly sawn edge.

Idea: For wooden shelves of high quality to display art and sculpture, use birch plywood rather than fir. Birch, with less grain than fir, takes a fine paint finish after sealing. . . .
Idea: It is possible to control fluorescent lighting with a dimmer so that lights can be used for both display and mood. (To install a dimmer, you must change the transformer.)

art in a library

Top left: A small hallway that doubles as a library is also display space for its owner's collection of Max Ernst lithographs. The works are randomly arranged and attached by hinges to allow browsers to reach books without taking down the frames. Interior designer: Piero Castellini.

art in a sitting room

Left: A stair-stepped unit in a sitting room is covered half in velvet for seating, half in shiny black plastic laminate for display of favorite photographs and *objets d'art*. The space beneath the steps could easily be used for further storage. Interior designer: Piero Castellini.

art in a living room

Above: Recesses flanking a decidedly modern fireplace are turned into miniature galleries with the addition of low double shelves on either side. Sculpture rests on the shelves, drawings and paintings against the wall. Uncomplicated lines and the use of all white make the space especially suited to the display of art. Recessed overhead lighting can be aimed to illuminate the top shelf. The lower shelf could also be fitted with similar lighting or equipped, as here, with separate eyeball lights. Designer: Piero Pinto.

Idea: Install conventional metal shelf standards at close, even intervals. Items to be stored—in clear plastic containers for visibility—can be fitted with hooks and hung in the standards like shelf brackets.

a place for everything

This masterpiece of open storage in a combined living room and study was specially designed not only to organize and protect its owner's possessions but also to display them. Some are works of art; others are treated so. One long fireplace wall is a honeycomb of adjustable cells and compartments, each engineered to fit the item stored: drums for photographic slide carousels, cylinders for plans, boxes for projectors. Architect: William J. Conklin.

1: Through remodeling, four tiny rooms became one, with one long wall given totally to storage. 2: A collection of antique Peruvian textiles, stretched on frames, are hung in compartments. 3: A stepladder designed by architect Conklin stands like sculpture near the fireplace but can be easily moved on ball bearings. 4: An 1862 niche, preserved in the remodeling, is filled with books. Blue plastic sunshades protect hanging textiles from ultraviolet light. 5: A freestanding file cabinet holds textiles and divides living and working areas. The top is carpeted for seating. 6: Clear plastic drums and white-painted wooden boxes hold photographic equipment. White plastic horseshoe-shaped boxes have transparent tops and bottoms for easy identification of their contents. All units clip on and off wall frames for convenience and flexibility. 7: Plastic cylinders hold plans and blueprints. 8: Books rest on even rows of plastic dowels rather than on solid shelves. This arrangement remains flexible, and requires only minimal dusting.

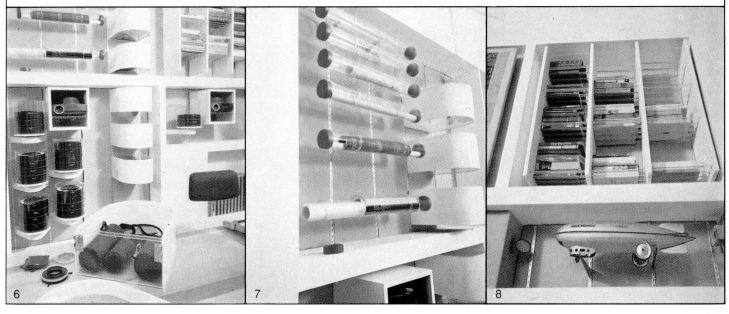

wine storage in a kitchen island

A massive kitchen island covered with brilliantly colored tiles is
large enough to hold more than one hundred bottles of wine in
its side. The built-in rack, constructed of single boards with
wood strips for guiders, holds the bottles perfectly horizontally.
Interior designer: Filippa Naess. Architect: Keith Kroeger.

Idea: Construct the base for a tiled cooking
island of wood framing and plywood sheathing,
allowing for electrical outlets and the wine rack.
After the plywood has been sealed, apply mastic
and tile directly to the base. Special instructions
are necessary when the island includes a cook-
top, electric or gas.

on racks in a basement

Below: Rows of shelves like library stacks hold jars of preserves in the basement of a remodeled farmhouse. Pin-and-dowel wine racks fit into a recess in the wall and reach the full height of the room. Most experts consider a cool underground room the best place to store wines (and preserves) for long periods of time. This library arrangement makes the most of limited cellar space handsomely. Architect: Charles Morris Mount.

ERNST BEADLE

HORST P. HORST

in clay pipes
in a cellar

Left: Space for this wine cellar was blasted out of rock when the house above it was first built. A medieval touch: a mass of rock remains in one corner. Wine bottles rest in a honeycomb of short terra cotta pipes set in concrete. Both of these materials are especially suited for keeping wine at the appropriate cool temperatures. Architect: Roland Terry.

JOHN FULKER

Idea: For a terra cotta wine rack, buy flue and drain tiles at a masonry supply outlet. (Such tiles come in appropriate sizes and do not require cutting.) Stack the tiles between supports made of heavy 1-inch drainpipe, threaded into flanges and screwed to wood planks top and bottom.

bottle storage in the city

Above: In a tiny city kitchen, previously wasted space under a counter was claimed for storage of bottled drinks of all kinds—mineral water, soda, tonic, wine. The device itself is a wooden grid, painted with high-gloss white enamel paint for easy care. A similar rack for short-term wine and liquor storage hangs on the wall.

wine storage in the country

Right: Terra cotta drainpipes are stacked in a rectangular block, secured with iron bands, and topped with wood to form a wine rack that also serves as a sideboard. For a kitchen, a slab of butcher block could be used on top, in which case the wine rack could do double duty as an extra chopping and working counter.

5
Decorative Storage

Closet doors faced with mirror—
Storage behind a fantasy
stage set—A plinth with
hidden shelves—Trompe-l'oeil
painting for cabinets—
Grillework for bookshelves—
Color graphics for cabinets and
shelves—Reflective surfaces
and dramatic lighting—
Materials for unexpected color
and texture—Lattice doors
that conceal a kitchen

For all the practicality of a well-planned storage system, what is its worth if it is not a joy to see? We can easily replace the ugly bulk of possessions in disarray with the bulk of the device used to contain it, but there is one consideration that makes all the difference: Is the containment an aesthetic improvement? Of course, all the storage ideas in this book have been chosen because they do the job *and* please the eye. But in this chapter, the purely visual concerns merit closer examination.

Like all elements in a room, storage becomes part of a very personal environment. The same techniques that are used to create these settings—color, light, texture, form—can be applied to the design of the storage pieces, whether they are considered by themselves or as integral parts of a total picture. Given the limiting requirements we have, more is possible than you might first imagine.

We sometimes classify storage as handsome or finely crafted or elegant. Imagine the possibilities of avant-garde, or cheering, or witty. Some storage is more important for how it looks than for what it does. Its very reason for existing might be one great decorative idea. One designer, inspired by the stage sets of the Teatro Olimpico in Vicenza, designed and had built a miniature street of classical façades that later became a row of closet doors. Trompe-l'oeil paintings on cabinets fall into the same category: their first function is to amuse and delight.

Color is perhaps the most powerful decorative tool. It can turn a storage piece into the graphic punch of a room. Lighting can be equally potent. At one end of the spectrum of its possibilities, it can simply illuminate display shelves. At the other end, it can transform a space into a spectacular walk-in still life—especially dramatic when lighting is used in combination with mirror and other reflective surfaces. Storage offers tremendous potential—to decorate a room, to be itself decorated.

mirrored closet doors

In a small space that is sometimes a dining room, sometimes a living room, mirrored folding doors across a full wall of closets brighten and expand the space and conceal materials used in the room's quick-change act. Split-level storage provides a place for dining chairs that are lovely to look at but in the way when the room is used for small groups. Another storage device, the mirrored tabletop is hung on the wall when the space becomes a living room. Architect: Alberto Pinto.

FRED LYON

a stage-set street for a dressing room

Above right: So extraordinary is this miniature fantasy street, the fact that it
is also an extremely efficient clothes closet is almost incidental. The room
itself is a dressing room. Each classical facade is a closet door with mirrors
for windows, and each opens out to reveal specialized storage behind it
(view with doors open, right). In one part, shirts slip into slots like letters into
pigeonholes. At one end of the wall is a lamp that serves as a valet. Interior
designer: John Dickinson.

plinths that turn to reveal hidden storage

Above left: In the same apartment whose dressing room is shown above
right, tall plinths of white-painted wood turn around to reveal shelves for
books and stereo equipment. The Roman emperors atop them are part
of the ploy: they are absolutely lightweight, made of papier-mâché.

color backing bookshelves

In one large room for living and entertaining, a warm hue painted on the back wall of recessed bookshelves adds a splash of color to a mostly white space and helps set apart a section of the room for reading and conversation. Another panel of color in the dining ell is a backdrop for sculpture displayed on a buffet cabinet. Interior designer: John F. Saladino. Architects: Philip Ives Associates.

grillework in front of bookshelves

Built-in bookcases that reach to the ceiling have doors faced with fine wire grilles for a traditional, rather masculine study. Existing cabinets with solid doors might be converted to this style by replacing the old doors with frames on hinges and fitting the frames with grillework attached on the hidden side. Old cases that once had glass in the doors might also gain a new look with grilles instead of glass. Designer: Stanley Falconer.

Idea: For a lazy-Susan storage plinth like the one shown opposite, use a potter's circular ball-bearing ring as a base.... **Idea:** Use expanded metal from industrial supply catalogues for library-cabinet grillework. For the finest finish, the grilles should be mortised into the doors.

TOM YEE

JAMES MORTIMER

color graphics for every storage element in a room

The bright-yellow cylinder of the lavatory cabinet provides the first big dose of color for a dressing room—bathroom. The same vivid primary on the back wall of open, sculptured shelves and on painted closet doors turns the room into one bold color graphic. One reason for its success: like an artist's canvas, the shell of the room is white. Architects: Robert Stern and John Hagmann.

Idea: If trompe-l'oeil paintings cover real cabinets, use pressure catches instead of hardware. . . . **Idea:** For large sliding doors that are also canvases for graphics, use rolling barn-door hangers.

trompe-l'oeil painting for the illusion of storage

In an alcove off a long central hallway, a playful, masterful trompe-l'oeil painting covers the walls and doors with pretend storage. The only real storage in this room is behind a closet door to the left (with a knob beneath the painted bust). Another door opposite this one leads to a bathroom, the open door to a bedroom. Architects: I. W. Colburn and Associates. Painting by Martin Newell.

color, proportion, and line

Above: Color is a subtle embellishment in a living room of pure architectural line. Massive posts of mellow green stand on either side of a dropped ceiling that gives great impact to the fireplace. They also support glass shelves that hold books and sculpture. Architect: Alberto Pinto.

reflection and sculpture

Below: The entire dining room and its row of cabinets pictured at the right are captured on the copper surface of an enormous discoid sculpture by Gilioli. Light reflected from the sculpture, as well as from the mirrored storage piece, burnishes the room.

light and transparency

Left: At the opposite end of the living room pictured across the page, lighting plays a great role in achieving an elegant, tranquil setting. Most of the illumination comes from uplights in opposite corners. The storage piece, an acrylic plastic display case for artifacts, is especially effective when used with a well-staged lighting scheme. While the case is basically transparent, light makes the plastic edges an electric white, so that the piece, as it stands in the room, becomes a rather sophisticated study in intersecting lines in space.

light and reflection

Below left: A dining room seems filled with a rich bronze glow as light reflects from mirrored recesses in a row of deep-brown cabinets. The recesses, designed for displaying sculpture, are lighted from above. An uplight in a corner provides more general illumination. All of the rich color and dramatic lighting are reflected in a giant discoid sculpture (far left.)
Architect: Alberto Pinto.

Idea: When building with acrylic plastic (see the transparent display case, opposite top), use screws as well as cement to hold the piece together. First drill a slightly undersized pilot hole, then use a tap to thread the hole for the permanent machine screw. An alternative method is to heat a flathead wood screw with a torch (holding it with pliers), and then to force the very hot screw into the predrilled hole, using a screwdriver.

unexpected color in a kitchen

Windows in unconventional places splash this vacation-house kitchen with light. Storage design for the room does the same thing with color. Juxtaposed with warm wood tones for the walls and earthy terra cotta for the floor, soft purple for the cabinets, shelves, and appliance fronts is an unexpected delight. Although all of these surfaces could easily be plastic laminate, which is available in an almost unlimited color selection now, they could also be painted with easy-to-wash paint, as these are. Interior designer: Jane Bell. Architect: Brett Donham.

a surprise of color in a living room

Above: Furniture is grouped around a built-in cabinet and console unit for books and stereo equipment as it might be around a fireplace in a more traditional setting. But the real surprise, and the feature that sets this music and library corner off from the rest of the room, is the use of flower blue for the entire wall—shelves, cabinets, and counters. For the easiest maintenance, such a unit should be sheathed in plastic laminate. For the least expense, it could be finished with the same semigloss paint that is ordinarily used for woodwork. Interior designer: painter Piero Sadun.

Idea: For economy, use plastic laminates only on the front-facing surfaces of open cabinets. Inside surfaces can be painted. To match colors, choose the laminate first, then have paint mixed to match in either high-gloss or semigloss enamel, depending on the finish of the laminate.

color in an all-purpose room

Below: Bright red and blue plastic laminates were used to sheathe cabinets and appliance fronts on the kitchen wall of a living-dining-cooking room. The house is a second home, built out on a promontory with a commanding view of the ocean. The location also means that exterior paint would wear very quickly (the wood sheathing of the house is treated with a clear preservative instead), so most color is concentrated inside. Architect: John Fowler.

NIMATALLAH

painted iron and plexiglass

Left: In a London kitchen, remodeling included stripping down
the walls to the original Georgian brick and adding a
long-wished-for stove called an Aga cooker. To emphasize the
heavy design of the stove, its big iron doors were painted
yellow and more iron doors were sought out to cover the fronts
of cabinets and drawers. In startling contrast are the
fragile-looking plexiglass cabinets high above the work area.

folding lattice doors

Above: An entire kitchen is hidden behind a system of folding
doors in a room that is streamlined and warm at the same time.
With the doors closed, the decorative latticework has the
appearance of highly styled wood paneling, and the room
becomes an elegant space for dining. With the doors open, a
striking stainless steel kitchen is revealed. A hood with
exhaust fans protects the wood from steam and smoke. More
doors to the left conceal spacious pantries. Kitchen
system is designed by Cordero.

Idea: To make doors with a grid
design similar to those shown above,
use a table saw. Run parallel dado
cuts across the top face of a plywood
panel, then turn the panel around and
make cross-cuts in the opposite direc-
tion. Make sure each cut goes more
than halfway through the wood.

6
Storage Devices

Old-fashioned hutches —
Contemporary cupboards —
Secretaries and sideboards for
collection display — Armoires —
Chests of drawers — Lockers
for closets — Plywood blocks —
Pegboard and hooks —
Hanging hooks for pots and
pans and other equipment —
Sculpture-like book towers —
Canvas and pipe devices

Stratagems is another word for the devices you see on these several pages, for each device is the materialization of one great scheme for coping with objects. An ancient and never-to-become-obsolete device is one large piece of furniture to organize, protect, and conceal possessions. The idea, of course, is that a mass of unorganized objects is neither attractive nor easy to use, whereas a piece of furniture can be. The execution and use of each design are subject to almost limitless possibilities.

One obvious stratagem is to seek out an old piece and use it exactly as it was intended to be used: an eighteenth-century sideboard for an eighteenth-century dining room, or an old armoire in place of closets in a bedroom. Old pieces can be updated for modern living: a sink in a kitchen cupboard, lights in a corner secretary. Finding a new use for an old piece is as good as discovering a new device. Many antique cabinets make wonderful display cases with their doors left open and drawers pulled out. If you don't mind drilling through the back for wires, such cabinets are fine disguises for stereos.

For today's interiors, old formulas can be reinterpreted. A sleek freestanding cupboard that reaches the high, sloping ceiling of a modern room qualifies as architectural storage — an appropriate evolution. The same is true of an extended cupboard that divides a room. Contemporary storage furniture makes use of a wider range of materials and often takes inspiration from a wider range of design traditions. Significant among these is industrial storage design. Some totally new one-large-piece devices have been developed by contemporary designers: huge cubes for closets, sculpture to hold books.

And devices are not limited to single pieces of furniture, for a device can also be one great idea. A prominent example: hanging objects directly on the wall, or on pegboard, or from the ceiling, or from an overhead rack. Baskets, such efficient storage devices on their own, also need to be stored themselves, and hanging is a superb answer. Anything, in fact, that both works and pleases the eye is an answer — a fine stratagem — a well-devised device.

time-honored solutions

Two devices are at work in this old Italian country kitchen. First, that most traditional device of all, a cupboard. Second, a great idea: hanging the paraphernalia of cooking directly on the kitchen wall — in this case, a rather spectacular collection of fine copper cookware, an ancient stone wall.

DRUETTO

a contemporary cupboard defines a space

Left: While the traditional cupboard generally stands against a wall, the modern version can stand anywhere. This one, its clean lines and curves covered with black plastic laminate and chrome, has its place in the center of a large room, where it holds magazines and journals and also helps define a seating area. Designer: Giotto Stoppino.

Idea: For ready-cut, lightweight wood for building room dividers, use inexpensive hollow-core doors. Remember that because they are hollow, they cannot be significantly altered in size, though if necessary, they may be reduced by up to one inch on one side. Join the doors together with angle braces.

an extended cupboard divides a room

Two views above: The idea of using one large piece of furniture for storage need not be limited to large rooms. Here, one of the biggest devices serves one of the smallest spaces: a one-room apartment. In a room of these dimensions, such a unit borders on the architectural—evidence of the range of possibilities for one large device. Designer: Dal Lago.

LOUIS REENS

one large piece for a modern setting

The formula for this storage device is an old one: cabinets below, open shelves above. The interpretation is decidedly contemporary: a tall piece designed to stand in the center of a room and meet the angle of a sloping ceiling, its spare modern lines brightened with colorful graphics. Architect: Hans Kriek. Designer: Angelo Petrozelli.

Idea: Frame a floor-to-ceiling cupboard with 1 × 12 planks, back it with ¼-inch hardboard or plywood. Paint the back and shelves before attaching them to the 1 × 12 framing.... **Idea:** Use contact paper as masking when painting curving graphics.

JAY STEFFY

ERNST BEADLE

a secretary
used for display

Above left: The doors—even one drawer—of this finely made old Spanish secretary are left open, partly to show off its craftsmanship, partly to display the collection of minerals, shells, and artifacts it contains.

a traditional
side cupboard

Above right: In a restored eighteenth-century dining room, a beautiful old Delaware side cupboard is used just as it was intended to be used. The doors swing open to reveal an array of Mocha and Bennington ware to be used at the table with pewter, bone-handled cutlery, and iron candlesticks.

an old hutch
updated for today

Left: The kitchen of a restored Colonial farmhouse belongs to two periods. An authentically painted New England hutch for pewter and stoneware crocks has been updated with the modern conveniences of double stainless steel sinks and electrical outlets without losing its historic charm.

JAY STEFFY

an antique-market find: a French armoire

Above: An old answer to clothes storage, the armoire, is often overlooked for rooms that are not strictly period. For a new bedroom done in light woods and wicker, the dark and ponderous-looking finish of this French piece was stripped down to the bare oak.

a flea-market find: a cigar-box chest

Left: In a glassed-in dining porch just steps away from the kitchen, a flea-market chest with cigar-box drawers holds miscellaneous items for cooking on the kitchen side, for dining on the porch side. Some families divide up the drawers of such finds among them and use them to file away keys, receipts, recipes, warranties, business cards, laundry instructions, letters — almost anything.

Idea: Revamp old working cabinets with new pulls or hardware.... **Idea:** In both old and new cabinets, solve the problem of drawers that stick by sanding down the trouble spots and spraying them with a silicone sliding agent. If drawers are too loose, build them up with epoxy paste mixed with dry pigment to match the wood.

lockers in an exercise room

Right: Industrial supply companies are an unexpectedly fertile source of well-made, functional storage devices that can be used in houses and apartments as well as in the factories, schools, hospitals, and warehouses they were originally intended for. In a spectacular bath and exercise room, a row of gym lockers provides storage for jump ropes and weights in one section, towels in another, warm-up clothes in another, and so on. Interior designer: François Arnal.

lockers as a bathroom graphic

Left above: In another bath and exercise room, a new wall was framed to hold a row of lockers that is decorative as well as efficient. Within the frame of the yellow wall, each locker is a progressively deeper shade of green. Lockers can be fitted with extra shelves (they come with one near the top) to hold toiletries. Interior designer: François Arnal.

lockers as a bedroom closet

Left below: Lockers retain their originally intended, functional good looks when adapted for use as a bedroom closet in the apartment whose bathroom is shown above. For delicate clothing, the rough inner edges of recycled lockers should be masked with tape, or the entire locker lined with quilted fabric. Interior designer: François Arnal.

HENRY CLARKE

Idea: Buy used lockers from school or factory demolition sales, sand them and paint them with rust-proof paint.... **Idea:** Order new lockers from industrial supply catalogues.... **Idea:** If lockers are to rest directly on the floor, level them with shims from a lumberyard.... **Idea:** Equip one locker in the bathroom with a real lock to create a child-proof medicine cabinet.

DAVID MASSEY

huge plywood storage blocks

Above and small view opposite: Six massive sky-blue blocks on casters are both art and storage in a factory space converted to an apartment. Each plywood block, put together with glue and screws, is 5 feet high to accommodate clothes on hangers, 4 feet wide on the sides. To create two separate closets on opposite sides, each unit is divided down the middle. One block is fitted with rods for clothes, others with shelves for books, linens, and dishes; some are left as is for folding chairs and large equipment. Because there are no dividing walls in the apartment, the storage blocks also serve as space definers. Designer: Charles Amato.

more solid geometry for closets

Two views, right: In a room of solid geometric forms and dazzling primary colors, a long blue storage wall is actually a chain of three individual closets that are attached on the inside. Behind the hinged doors, wine, china, coats, even a Ping-Pong table, are stored. The entire wall can be moved on casters (the square holes on either end are handles). The room is full of ingenious and decorative storage devices. High on the far wall (top view), a yellow frame holds projection equipment. Along one wall, a red case holds canvas window shades. The brightly striped cylinder conceals an I-beam. Interior designer: Merrill Scott. Architect: Yann Weymouth.

TOM YEE

Idea: For one 4-by-4-by-5-foot storage block (left), use six standard 4-by-8-foot sheets of plywood for minimum waste. Saw one sheet in half for the top and bottom; trim the remaining five sheets for the 4-by-5-foot sides and central divider. Use excess plywood for shelves. . . . **Idea:** Paint the interior of storage blocks with high-gloss enamel paint for easy maintenance.

111

ERNST BEADLE

kitchen equipment against brick

Above: In an old-fashioned-looking kitchen, traditional brick was used for the stove, oven, and chimney structure in the center of the floor, providing an ideal display and storage wall for hanging kitchen equipment. A masonry drill and anchors must be used to fasten hooks in the wall, but if you change your mind about placement, the rough texture of the brick helps conceal the holes.

a collection hung on pegboard

Right: A splendid collection of baskets and kitchen gadgets is stored and displayed with great appeal on two full walls of pegboard. Flexibility is perhaps the greatest asset of pegboard. The holes are already there, in a pattern of their own, so displays can be changed again and again. These pegboard walls are even more flexible than they first appear, for they are actually hinged in 4-by-8-foot sections to a larger panel that can be rolled around on casters. Designer: Richard Pratt.

Idea: To install a wall of pegboard, first have the panels cut to measure at the lumberyard. (They come in 4-by-8-foot sheets.) At home, apply 1×2 furring strips to the wall with screws (for even walls) or with panel adhesive (for less even walls), then nail the pegboard to the furring strips. Without the space created by the furring strips, it is impossible to insert hooks in the pegboard.

ERNST BEADLE

pots and pans hanging from a ceiling rack

Left: When searching for storage space, the first place one usually looks is on the wall, and then, perhaps, in the center of the floor. The ceiling's potential for storage is often neglected. To make use of this space, one great storage device is also a simple one: hang attractive items within easy reach overhead. In this kitchen, an iron rack suspended from the ceiling provides all the space needed for a full battery of pots and pans. Hang the most frequently used pots closest to the cooking area, not only for convenience but also because the most used are the most washed and therefore less likely to accumulate grease from cooking vapors.

baskets hanging from ceiling beams

Above: Timbers in the ceiling provide ready-made hanging racks. Only a few nails and perhaps some S-hooks are required to hang a collection of baskets. Nothing very weighty should be stored inside. Good candidates for a setting such as this one: chestnuts near the fireplace, knitting or needlework by a comfortable chair.

Idea: To hang especially heavy objects, like the pot rack shown opposite, use threaded iron waterpipe and flanges screwed directly into the ceiling framing.... **Idea:** Hang baskets from wooden pegs rather than nails; wood is easier on the baskets and nicer to look at than raw metal.

DEREK BUTLER

a straw pyramid for magazines

Above: Straw, an unexpected material for large storage devices, was used to create a pyramid for magazine storage that is at once elegant and witty. Pockets on all four sides of the form hold magazines—or any light item one might wish to display. Interior designers: Stefano Mantovani and Verde Visconti.

a sculpture that holds books

Left: A bookshelf-tower of white-lacquered wood stands like sculpture in a spare, all-white living room. Such a piece could easily hold its own in the center of the room. It must be placed some distance from the wall, as shelves extend from both sides. Designer: Ugo La Pietra for Poggi.

ALDO BALLO

canvas and pipe devices

Below: For living and storage furniture for an entire room, lightweight steel pipes and canvas were combined to make a bunk bed with storage pockets at one end, a cantilevered desk and chair, a rolling mail cart, and an étagère. Using a pocketed panel at the end of a bed is an idea that could be adapted for almost any bunks. Furniture components by Roche-Bobois.

Idea: For a finer finish for plastic-laminate-sheathed constructions, use the thinnest laminate available: the thinner the laminate, the less visible the edge on corners. However, remember that thin laminate does not hold up to wear as well as the thicker, less elegant version.

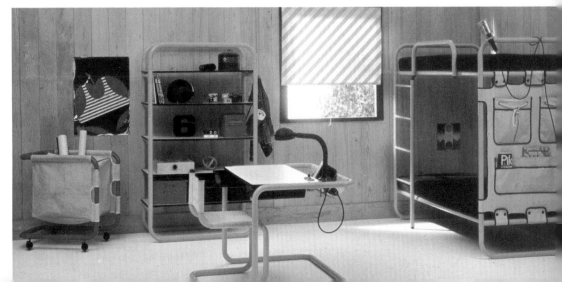

7
Kitchen Storage

Pegboard on the wall—
A specialized system for one
kitchen—Cabinets of wood,
plastic laminate, stainless steel—
Sleek line and bold color for
kitchen storage—
Glass-fronted cabinets—
Plastic-laminate cabinets
combined with mirror, with
wood—Storage for a galley
kitchen—Open and closed
shelves combined—
Kitchen-island storage—
A room-dividing grid of
shelves—Glass shelves for
glasses—Cabinets and shelves
for special spaces

There are two basic philosophies behind kitchen design. One: The kitchen is a laboratory and should be clean and uncluttered. Two: The kitchen is a creative den and should have the look of a master craftsman's shop. In practice, the two philosophies often come down to a simple difference in storage design: closed versus open cabinets. Both approaches offer considerable flexibility, and of course, it is possible to combine them.

If you choose closed cabinets, there are the front-facing materials to consider—light wood, dark wood, painted wood, plastic laminates. Color and hardware must be considered as well, and what is to be behind those closed doors. Most kitchen-planning experts agree that it is not the number of cabinets you have that makes the difference but how well they are planned to accommodate what you own. The best solution is to have storage units in a variety of dimensions—full-length cabinets as well as short ones, deep drawers as well as shallow. Specialized cabinets can be a joy, with shelves that pull or swing out for pots and pans and appliances.

Open storage requires a willingness to keep everything constantly presentable. Well-planned open systems begin with a place for each item—a built-in order that is easy to maintain—whether on shelves, pot racks, pegboards, or ledges. Narrow over-the-counter shelves can hold alphabetized spices; display-case shelves can hold foods arranged by color; glass shelves can be built to hold nothing but glasses.

Perhaps for the kitchen more than anywhere else, placement of storage is of crucial importance. In addition to the usual places on empty walls, space for storage can be claimed above doors, around windows, under islands, on the ceiling. One excellent way to determine the best place to store things is to draw a map of your work areas, then trace your movements as you pace through recipes you frequently use. Where are you when you need mixing bowls, the blender, flour, cooling racks? Place cupboards and shelves accordingly. When kitchen storage fits both your space and your style, more than efficiency is the reward.

a pegboard organizer

Serious cooks with large *batteries de cuisine* have long known the convenience of hanging utensils within easy reach. In this professional-style kitchen, utensils become hanging *objets d'art*—pleasing to look at and simple, at eye level, to reach. The pegboard extends the length of the counter it serves, with implements grouped basically by function: rolling pin and pastry brush nearest the pastry board, for example. One trick for easy maintenance of the system: each piece of equipment is outlined on the pegboard in black. Owners/designers: Julia and Paul Child.

HORST P. HORST

a system of specialized storage

Meticulous planning is the key to the most efficient kitchen storage systems. The two-step program for the kitchen shown on these two pages began with dividing the space into three functional areas: a food preparation center (opposite), a pantry and clean-up zone (detail below right), and a laundry (just past the cooking island, left). All equipment and materials involved in each activity zone are stored right there. The second step was to specialize the individual cabinets and drawers for each specific area. The good looks of the room come from the use of fine materials rather than from many decorative elements—stainless steel for lower cabinets, briarwood pecan for upper cabinets and walls, maple butcher block for counter tops. Designer: Bernard Sucher of St. Charles Kitchens.

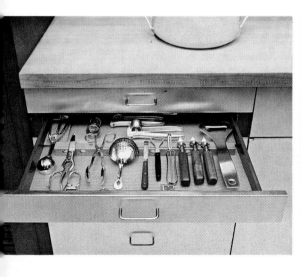

Idea: For a new kitchen, list what you have to store and where you want to put it (near the refrigerator, near appliance plug-ins, etc.) before you choose cabinets. . . . **Idea:** For an old kitchen, specialize existing storage with dividers, trays, magnetic bars, pegboard for drawers, new shelves and pull-out trays for cabinets.

Left and above left: Drawers for knives and other skinny utensils were designed to be very shallow to eliminate the need to dig to the bottom. Magnetic bars, often used on the wall, keep the drawers tidy. Above center: One cabinet is fitted with extremely shallow pull-out trays for napkins and placemats, organized by size and color.

graphic line, bold color

Above and right: The storage structures are a blaze of shiny white against walls and floor of deep glossy blue — cabinets and shelves as important for their color and line as for their efficiency. A double tier of open shelves turns the corner and holds decorative and often-used condiments and equipment. Easy-to-clean blue plastic panels back the shelves; a strip of chrome trims the lower counters. Above one long black marble counter is a special niche for cookbooks. Designer: Aldo Jacober.

ERNST BEADLE

streamlined efficiency

Four views above: For a serious cook, cabinets and drawers on three sides of the room and beneath a center island provide the required superorganization. Dimensions of the units vary for greatest efficiency; cabinets above and below the counter are combined with full-height pantries along two walls. (One pantry wall has a pass-through to the dining room.) For a handsome, streamlined look: unfussy black surfaces, all equipment under cover. Architects: Lundquist and Stonehill. Planners: St. Charles Kitchens.

Idea: To increase the efficiency of a full wall of floor-to-ceiling cabinets, fit at least one with narrow shelves on all three inside walls. Narrow shelves make it easier to see what you have, what you need to reorder. . . . **Idea:** To further specialize specialized cabinets and drawers, arrange things in alphabetical order (spices, soups, appliance warranties).

ERNEST BRAUN

salvaged treasures for a new kitchen

Left: In a remodeled townhouse, an old passageway in the
basement became a new kitchen. Inspired by the vaulted
ceiling, the design is old-world and charming, with many of the
storage solutions provided by travel finds and objects
salvaged from old buildings: stained-glass cabinet fronts from
an old apartment, a hanging scale from an olive market in
Sicily, a bird-shaped pulley from a wellhead in Spain,
a cubbyhole cabinet from a demolished building.
Architects: Adolf de Roy Mark and Girvin Kurtz.

new treasures with an old look

Above: The warmth of wood gives this kitchen much of its
character. All the cabinets are stained oak; one counter is
butcher block. Glass-fronted cabinets and tiles are part of the
country-kitchen look. A high shelf provides space for storage
above a large window. Interior designer: Helen Dryfous.
Architect: Herbert D. Kosovitz.

Idea: Even in kitchens where all space
seems to be occupied, it is often possible to increase storage space by adding a single shelf here and there—
above a door, across a window, below a
cabinet. Use angle braces for support.

TOM YEE

Idea: To clean plastic laminate, use spray cleaner and a soft cloth, never scouring powder, which could scratch the surface.... **Idea:** Use plastic mirror squares, available in hardware and department stores, to cover the walls behind shelves or sink splashbacks.

plastic laminate and mirror

Above: Materials chosen for cabinets and open storage make all the difference in this small (15-foot-square) kitchen. Ultramarine blue plastic laminate covers cabinets, shelves, range hood, and appliance fronts. Mirror behind the glass shelves and high-up blue shelf brightens and expands the space. Note mirror trim on the under-counter cabinets. Interior designers: William Machado and Norman Diekman.

plastic laminate and wood

Right: Traditional above-and-below-the-counter cabinets are again untraditionally executed to combine two approaches: the time-tested arrangement is for efficiency; the innovative design is for visual appeal. These matte black plastic-laminate cabinets vary in dimensions for versatility, the tallest reaching clear to the ceiling. Open shelves of light-toned wood are integrated into the system. Architect: Claudio Dini.

a system for a tiny galley

Above: In a small galley kitchen, open shelves on three sides of the room supplement under-counter cabinets. Along the solid wall, a shelf covered with white plastic laminate conceals lighting beneath it. Above cabinets that form a partial room divider, a narrow counter can be used for storage as well as work space. Along the glass wall, shelves claim a wall for storage without destroying the view.

a system for a large room

Right: A peninsula with a butcher-block top not only increases this kitchen's counter space but also provides more space for cabinets. All here are painted black. Open shelves above one work area hold frequently used dishes and baskets that have almost unlimited storage potential. They could hold cutlery, linens, onions, potatoes, even cleaning agents that are carried from room to room. Designer: Kipp Stewart.

Idea: Flush nautical hardware works as well in kitchens as it does on boats. It is convenient and handsome, and keeps cabinets free of protrusions near active areas. . . . **Idea:** Create a cooking peninsula by supporting a butcher-block slab with two cabinets. Choose the counter top first from stock sizes, build the cabinets to fit.

an open grid for a kitchen–living room

In this remodeled kitchen, entertainment space and cooking space are combined, which means that guests seated around a coffee table are nearer the cook for conversation and a new space is available to the kitchen for storage. A grid of shiny black painted shelves above a dining bar—open to both sides of the room—holds food staples, wines, and objects just to look at. Interior designer: François Catroux.

a design for an angular plan

Above: A built-in cabinet for a small angular kitchen was designed with angular lines and painted white to make it seem a mere extension of the wall. The front of the cabinet drops down to become a supplementary counter. Along the adjacent wall, narrow glass shelves store bottles and glasses out of the way of most traffic. Architects: Roy Stout and Patrick Litchfield.

a shelf over an island

Right: Tobacco-brown cabinets and drawers in specialized sizes line one wall and keep nearly everything under cover. One exception: a shelf above the cooking-dining island holds decorative items out of the way of the cook.

Idea: To build an open storage grid, frame a box of 1 × 12 planks, install horizontal shelves at even intervals, then wedge in vertical boards as dividers. A partial backboard made of ¼-inch hardboard adds strength.

open storage for limited space

In a long, narrow kitchen that is separated from a dining room only by a partial wall and two wide sets of louvered doors, pegboard and two over-the-door shelves make the most of minimal wall space (above). Heavy, professional-weight cookware goes on well-supported shelves, copper pans and pot lids hang on the pegboard, other utensils swing from hooks attached to the undersides of the shelves. Right: On the opposite wall, a narrow shelf just below the cabinets holds spices where they are readily accessible but clear of work areas. Owner/designer: Michael Field.

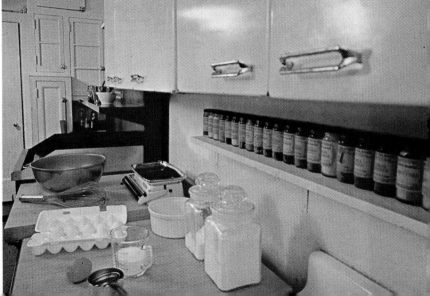

TOM YEE

remodeling for more storage

Above: Made-to-measure cabinets and shelves hold an abundance of equipment in a large remodeled cellar kitchen. One wall is lined with floor-to-ceiling, hardware-free wood cabinets that hide ugly and unnecessary basement windows. Arched, lighted niches display antique game-pie casseroles; copper molds hang from a fake beam that hides pipes. Beneath a polished marble pastry counter is a shelf for crocks of flour and grains. A bonus for this arrangement: the shelf protects a stretch of floor space for hard-to-store, hard-to-retrieve outsize items. Left: Across the room, hooks on a beam hold copper pans, magnetic bars hold knives. Interior designer: George Doan.

Idea: Use angle braces to support narrow under-cabinet shelves for spices.... **Idea:** A single bare incandescent bulb can be used to illuminate niches where an arched front panel masks the source of light.... **Idea:** For hanging pots and pans from wooden beams, use vinyl-coated screw hooks for least abrasion, use thick, rectangular-headed masonry nails for the look of a country kitchen.

133

8
Bedroom Storage

Platform beds — Headboard
shelf systems — Shelves
in niches — Closets between
niches, under a balcony —
A totally built-in bedroom —
Platforms for stoves and
storage — Stair-step closets —
Bedside bookshelves —
Color-coded storage blocks —
Bunk-bed storage —
Specialized closets —
Put-together components for a
child's room — Room-dividing
storage blocks — Wall storage —
Closets and shelves for
growing children

It has been said that for this century — and probably for all of those to follow — space is the greatest luxury. The idea extends all the way from the concept of a crowded planet to the more immediate problem of a crowded house, a crowded apartment. To many, true spatial luxury means plenty of room in that most personal spot of all, the bedroom. Carefully planning bedroom storage is a first step in making the most of the limited personal space we have.

The traditional answer has been traditional furniture — the three-piece suite or perhaps the wedding-present chest of drawers. More recently, newer — and older — ideas have been put into practice, turning bedroom design completely around. Notable among these new/old ideas is the platform bed, a contemporary interpretation of the old seaman's solution to storage, the captain's bed. The platform, with its large drawers that make under-bed storage easy to reach and easy to organize, can be the only furniture in the room, serving many needs. In other settings, it can be part of a system: everything in the room is built in, and the platform bed is an extension of other storage devices, such as bookshelves that serve as a headboard. Even bunk beds can be a form of platform bed, with one support column made into a full chest of drawers.

All of the approaches to storage in this book can be applied specifically to bedrooms. Shelving at bedside can take the place of night tables. Systems like the one described above can coordinate all the furniture and storage in the room. An architectural approach might include a sleeping loft with built-in storage tucked beneath it. New devices like stair-stepped closets make the best use of unusual spaces. One of the oldest devices, the bedroom closet, can gain new efficiency with a plan that organizes every inch.

Special solutions are required for those special rooms belonging to children. Adaptability is the key here. Because storage requirements change as children grow, the best systems are readily adapted — from toy storage, say, to clothing or book storage — and are sufficiently sturdy to last. Within this portfolio of bedrooms for both adults and children are ideas to inspire your own storage solutions.

a simple platform

In a room designed as a sparse sleeping chamber where nothing must detract from the drama of the architecture, a simple wooden platform serves both as furniture — bed, table, seating — and as a storage unit for clothing, linens, and even heavier items such as books or exercise equipment. Such a platform could be constructed of 2 × 3 framing covered with texture #111 plywood panels. The drawers are plywood boxes. Architect: Gae Aulenti.

a closet between two niches

The wide swing of a closet door can create space problems in small bedrooms. Here, a simple panel of fabric masks clothes storage between two built-in bookcases, eliminating the need to set aside "swing space." Clothes are readily accessible as the curtain is pushed aside, and the choice of fabric becomes a design element of the room. Window shades could be similarly used—in bamboo, matchstick, or venetian-style in decorator colors. Interior designer: Annig Sarien.

a wall niche filled with headboard storage

Niches in the wall are used to great advantage for the closet and limited headboard storage (opposite). A larger space (above) allows generous room for bookshelves that hold not only books but also a reading light and hard-to-store stereo equipment and records. The bed platforms are permanently attached to the bookshelf-headboard. A key design decision here: the shelves do not entirely fill the niche, allowing great flexibility in the use of the uppermost shelf. Interior designer: Annig Sarien.

Idea: To add both a closet and deep twin niches, build a new wall several inches out from an old one, using 2×4 studs to frame in the wall and niches. Cover the frame with plasterboard; tape and spackle nail holes before painting. Shelves can be supported with simple brackets.

built-ins under a balcony and in a bed

In a sleekly contemporary bedroom, a built-in storage complex sheathed in white plastic laminate serves as a closet, chest of drawers, and luggage cabinet. The high ceiling allows space for a seating balcony above the storage wall. (The bathroom, also below the balcony, is behind the storage complex.) Bookshelves are convenient but inconspicuous in components that form the head and foot of the built-in bed. Architect: Myron Goldfinger.

Idea: For a built-in bed like the one shown above, construct two boxes and a bedframe of ¾-inch plywood. (The two boxes can be fitted with shelves.) Bolt the three pieces together and cover the whole with plastic laminate....
Idea: Buy ladders and railings for storage lofts from nautical suppliers.

storage units stacked end to end

Below: Through remodeling, a nineteenth-century bedroom gained the decidedly modern look of all built-ins. Strong white forms continue around the room and seem to support each other, like building blocks. A plant shelf extends from wall to wall in front of the windows. High bookshelves hold professional journals; on their undersides are concealed lighting. More building blocks form the daybed, the bed, a table, and headboard consoles on either side of the whimsical fireplace. Architect: Warren Cox.

ERNST BEADLE

wood storage beneath a stove

Above: When a bedroom includes a fireplace or a Franklin
stove, one special storage challenge is finding a place for the
wood. In this master bedroom in a remodeled barn, a wooden
platform stretches the full width of the space. Firewood goes
underneath the platform, leaving the top free for other
storage and casual seating.

a system designed around a stove

Left: A brass-pipe stove that once warmed a small ship is one
showpiece in a rough-pine-paneled bedroom. A built-in
storage system is designed around it. The shelves hold books;
the platform becomes a banquette, a ledge for plants, a side
table for anyone seated near the fire. Above the entire setup,
downlights are recessed in the ceiling. Designer: Kipp Stewart.

Idea: When a stove stands on a
wooden platform, use a slab of slate or
stone beneath it for extra protection....
Idea: To safeguard against mold and
mildew, store only dry, well-seasoned
wood in the bedroom.

ACHIM DEILING OSTRINSKY

bedside bookshelves of industrial chrome

Left : The use of industrial components is unexpected but surprisingly handsome in an elegant bedroom. The idea is a simple one: bookshelves on either side of a bed require the same floor space as standard night tables but provide remarkably greater storage potential. Industrial components offer the advantages of strength, flexibility in the arrangement of shelves, and easy assembly.

a corner platform for an attic room

Right above: Inventive use of space made it possible to create a bedroom in a tiny attic corner. An equally inventive platform bed continues the efficient use of space. An L-shaped shelf, level with the mattress, is a headboard that doesn't waste minimal vertical space. Drawers on three sides of the platform make use of all the under-bed space.

engineered closets beneath the stairs

Right below: In a bedroom on a lower level, the usual dead space beneath the risers of the stairs is put to use for very specialized clothes storage. The shortest unit is divided with shelves; each progressively taller unit holds longer, taller items. (Square panels atop each closet serve as a geometric stair railing.) Within the first three steps: a flip-top toy box.

Idea: Stair-step storage closets to fit under a staircase or to stand free can be built of plywood and covered with ¼-inch hardboard. The hardboard provides a smooth surface for spray-painting and can be applied to allow a lip for the door, thus providing a tight seal.

CHRISTINA GHERGO

143

TOM YEE

a total storage system, color-coded

Above: Color signals function in a vivid bedroom where every bit of furniture is built in and every built-in designed for efficient storage. Blue is for clothes closets. Red is for cubes that contain a refrigerator and a television set and serve as a desk—all on casters so that they can be moved anywhere. Yellow is for drawers that store clothes, files, small equipment, and tapes for the nearby stereo. Interior designer: Merrill Scott. Architect: Yann Weymouth.

stacked beds, sliding drawers

Right: In exceptionally limited space, beds can be stacked in traditional nautical fashion. Drawers beneath the bottom bunk are best fitted with casters if items to be stored are heavy. If storage is limited to clothing or linens, drawers can be suspended from the bottom of the bed—easier to handle with a rug on the floor. Interior designer: Sylvia Owen. Architect: Christopher Owen.

Idea: For a long row of oversize drawers (above), build simple boxes of ½-inch plywood. Use an electric saber saw to cut hand-holes; mount the boxes on nylon drawer slides. The best steps for a smooth, glossy finish: sand, seal, sand, fill with spackle, sand, prime, sand—then spray with a few thin coats of bright enamel.

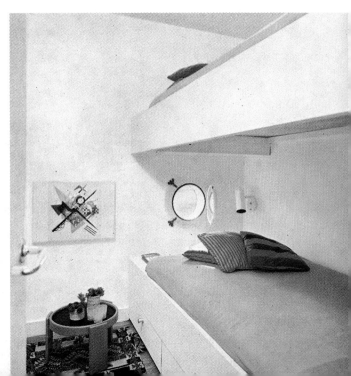

drawers plus headboard

Left: In the same color-coded bedroom pictured opposite, a massive geometric platform bed has oversize drawers that are suspended from the bedframe itself. The headboard is wired for permanent lamps. Interior designer: Merrill Scott. Architect: Yann Weymouth.

a bunk-bed bureau

Right: The ultimate in under-bed storage is possible with bunk beds. Here, perpendicular placement of the bunks makes the high stack of drawers easily accessible. Because the drawers pull out into the center of the room rather than into a corner, they can extend the full depth of the large supporting element. Architect: Brett Donham.

EMMETT BRIGHT

shelves in a living-bedroom

Above: In a living area that could also serve as a guest room (a special but frequent bedroom storage problem), shelves not only line the walls but, in one case, form a dividing wall. For guest storage, shelves behind the giant sofa are left empty. The bridge above connects a reading gallery with another small gallery that opens onto a terrace. Architect: Gae Aulenti.

ERNST BEADLE

Idea: Make inclined shelves for shoes of ¾-inch plywood with a 1 × 3 clear pine fascia strip for a stop front. To position, start with the lowest shelf, glueing and nailing it in place at a 30° angle. For each succeeding shelf, measure up 9 inches from the front and back of the shelf beneath.

space engineering for closets

More than size distinguishes an efficient clothes closet from an inefficient one. Specialization makes the most of the space available and assures that everything has a place that is easy to reach, easy to keep organized, well suited to the item stored. In one triumph of space planning (above), long rods hold a double row of suits and jackets, another rod is placed at a height to accommodate coats, and shoes fit onto sloping shelves. Designer: John F. Saladino. In another (right), clothing bags hung high hold out-of-season clothes, and trousers are hung on a rod below jackets. In both, chests of drawers and open shelves store folded items, handbags, boxes. Designers: Gordon-Locker Associates.

a take-apart,
put-together system

An entire wall of furniture — beds, drawers, cabinet, closet, desk, shelves — answers nearly all the living and storage needs a growing child could have. The greatest advantage of this system is its flexibility. Designed and constructed in components, it can be taken apart and rearranged as the child's interests, age, physical size — or room — changes. Made of fir plywood with a heavy-duty polyurethane finish that is easily wiped clean, these components are exceptionally durable — especially important for a child's room. Metal fasteners (part of the easy, knock-down feature of the system) are left exposed as part of the straightforward character of the design. Bookshelves are hung on simple T-shaped brackets. The closer together these are placed, the greater the weight they can support.

Idea: Use a stair rail (in stock at lumberyards) as a safety bar for a child's bed.... **Idea:** To retain the clean white look of freshly sawn wood, rub on a coat of white stain and allow it to dry before applying a poly-urethane finish.... **Idea:** If cabinet and drawer units are of the same dimensions, one can be more easily changed for the other if the need arises.

blocks for storage and room division

Two views below: In a dormitory playroom shared by three young brothers, storage design serves two important functions. First, it provides a variety of drawers, shelves, closets, toy bins, and overhead spaces to hold all the paraphernalia of a growing boy. Second, it divides the large room into three separate domains so that each boy gets his fair share of the space, his private places for his private stuff. Lest there be any doubt as to which compartment is whose, each one is marked with bright painted wood letters. Each block has a closet, drawers, and open shelves on one end, adjustable open shelves with plastic bins on one side, bunk beds (so each boy can have a visitor) on the other side. Because the blocks are less than ceiling height, the spaces are still open to one another. The top of each is extra storage space. Architect: John Russell Nichols.

wall-space storage

Above: A child's own world beneath the rafters—loft bed above, sitting room and playroom below—makes great use of wall space for organizing possessions. Shelves hold books and a television; a long, wall-hung bookcase holds toys; a guitar and a crash helmet are hung directly on the wall. A mobile shelf hangs from the ceiling, and shallow open boxes to carry around the room slide out of sight in a closet. Interior designer: Dorothy Tyoran. Architect: Peter Luscombe.

JAMES MORTIMER

low drawers and a counter

Above: To make it simpler for children to reach them, the many drawers in this room stretch long and low rather than high. They are small enough so that no drawer, even when filled with clothes, could ever be too heavy for a child to handle. A long counter stretches between this storage piece and another to provide a work and play counter, more space for storage. Interior designer: Jill Dufwa.

TOM YEE

brick and board shelving

Above: Building-block bricks and boards of heavy plastic are stacked to make shelves in the fashion of cinderblock and 2 × 4's. The material used makes these shelves colorful and easy to clean. The design can be changed simply by restacking.

adjustable children's closets

Left: The mud room of a modern New England farmhouse includes separate cubicles for each child's clothes—an excellent solution for clothing storage that could be adapted to bedroom closets for children. The shelves, with hooks or rods attached to their undersides, are adjustable and can be raised as the child grows taller. A railing keeps boots and shoes inside the closet and helps in putting them on. Architect: Edward Colwell Collins II.

Idea: Personalize storage blocks for children (opposite left) with names cut out of acrylic plastic. First draw the letters on large sheets of graph paper, then transfer the design to the backing of the plastic. Cut out the letters with a saber saw, sand the edges, and finish with acrylic polish. Attach the letters to the walls with panel adhesive.

9
Bathroom Storage

One large structure for tub,
lavatory, and storage—
A full wall of specialized closets—
An armoire in the bathroom—
Mirror, shiny laminates,
cork, wood, and glass for
storage devices—A niche
with glass shelves—Banquettes
with under-seat storage—
An étagère for towels

Not so long ago, the bathroom was a rarely mentioned little cubicle with three standard fixtures and not much to boast about. We required only that it be workable and allotted it very limited space. Today, bathroom design has seen quite a change, and we hear such terms as "dressing-room baths" and "personal spas." The bathroom has been promoted to a setting for personal pampering, a place where people actually go to spend time. It is often planned to include wardrobe storage and dressing space, soaking tubs and whirlpools, even exercise equipment. At the most extravagant end of the spectrum, bathrooms are full-sized rooms with saunas, indoor gardens, and entertainment equipment. At the other end, even modest bathrooms are given greater attention, with more thought devoted to comfort and efficient use of space. In both instances, storage design plays an increasingly important role.

For elaborate, sybaritic settings, specialized closets and cabinets must hold clothing and equipment—all the luxuries planned for the room. As the bathroom takes its place as a full-fledged room, designers are developing whole new storage ideas, such as the giant bath-and-storage cylinder shown opposite. Even smaller bathrooms must contain more efficient storage than ever before as more cosmetics and appliances for personal grooming are introduced.

An increasing number of materials can withstand splashes and high humidity—a development that eliminates one barrier to more adventurous design. Now old ideas like wood cabinets are made more practical with polyurethane coatings. New colors and finishes for plastic laminates are inspiring new approaches to design: bathrooms with great bands of color or spas totally sheathed in laminates with nonblistering finishes. Banquettes upholstered in waterproof fabrics conceal storage beneath them; stretches of mirror hide rows of closet doors. Furniture of molded plastic finds a special place in the bathroom—stacking storage cylinders, étagères for linens. Designs can be as indulgent as you wish, as the bathroom becomes a room for grooming, for physical fitness, for contemplation.

an everything cylinder

An enormous white cylinder with bands of vivid color dominates a bedroom-bath complex. One side contains the washbasin, the other the tub. Built into the cylinder are two sets of generous drawers that seem to be a continuation of the stripes that reach halfway around. Storage is color-coded: blue for cosmetics and toiletries, yellow for towels, red for miscellaneous necessities: hair dryers, loofahs, extra toilet rolls, a hand-laundry basket. Interior designer: Merrill Scott. Architect: Yann Weymouth.

reflective surfaces
mask a row of closets

Right: A sleekly contemporary dressing room and bath has the look of pure indulgence, but beneath the spectacular glitter is a well-planned, hard-working storage system. A row of five highly specialized closets lines the longest wall of the room. The doors of the closets and a medicine cabinet just to the left of the basin are covered with shiny brown plastic laminate, so that they meld into the general gleam of the room. Because surfaces in the room are so highly reflective (mirror covers the ceiling, backsplash, and cabinet front; bright oxidized aluminum surrounds the tub and basin), the closets do not stand out as a military row of doors. Clean-lined drawers without hardware are equally inconspicuous. Interior designer: François Catroux.

behind the doors:
superorganization, convenience

Above: The closets in the bathroom (opposite) are engineered to perfectly accommodate the items stored. Glass shelves in the medicine cabinet hold toilet articles, slide-out shelves in the wardrobe hold shirts (one or two to a shelf), racks hold a dozen pairs of shoes. Bulkier items are stored on the top closet shelf. Conventional clothes closets continue to the left, though one large space could be used for exercise equipment. Right: The same shiny brown doors conceal a toilet and bidet compartment.

ERNST BEADLE

Idea: For mirrored ceilings, use lightweight plastic rather than glass mirrors; apply with panel adhesive....
Idea: To clean large expanses of glass and mirror like an expert, use window cleaner and newspapers, which are lint-free and more absorbent than cloth. To avoid scratching, dust only with a damp cloth.

slate floor, tub, and cabinets

Below: In a house that was remodeled from a barn, a
12-by-15-foot space was set aside for a master bathroom
with an enormous sunken tub in the center of the floor.
The tub, like the rest of the floor, is covered in gray slate,
as is the double lavatory and cabinet unit that forms one
high wall of the tub. An unexpected and delightful luxury:
an antique armoire holds linens and clothes. Designer:
Richard Heinmann.

ERNST BEADLE

cork for walls and cabinet

Above: Another surprise for a bathroom: a cabinet completely sheathed in cork. The unit itself is striking for its efficiency—a combination of open storage, large drawers, and shallow drawers for make-up, combs, small toiletry articles that get lost in larger compartments. The entire room is lined with cork, so the storage unit, with its matching front, has the handsome look of custom furniture. Architects: Giuliano Guiducci and Mario Majoli.

Idea: To completely line a bathroom with cork, use tiles specially made for the purpose. Apply tile cement with a serrated trowel and press squares in place. Finish with a spray coating of protective silicone.

niches in a mirrored room

Above: A space-age bathroom with an abundance of sparkle
and gleam is also rich in storage space—hidden behind
mirrored doors. Mirrored niches with the streamlined shape of
airplane windows hold glass bottles; more storage space could
be claimed beneath the white vinyl banquette.
Interior designer: David Barrett.

Idea: Apply mirror panels to the wall with
panel adhesive, using a caulking gun to
shoot a dab every 6 inches. The mirror must
be supported for a few hours while the
cement dries. The larger the panel, the
thicker the mirror should be—1/16 inch for
small squares, 1/4 inch for a 4-by-8-foot
panel. When you buy the mirror, have any
edges that will be exposed ground smooth.

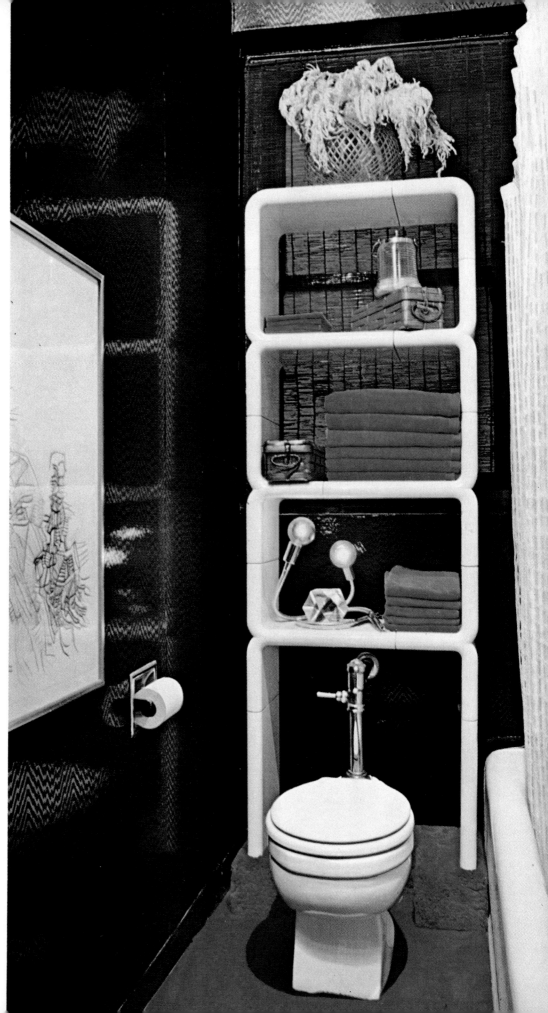

an étagère for linens above a fixture

Right: When bathroom space is extremely limited, one place to look for storage possibilities is above existing fixtures. For this sophisticated city bathroom, lots of natural light was not important. The window above the toilet was masked with a black-painted matchstick blind. In front of it, a white étagère holds towels and a lamp. Designer: Elaine Cohen.